MW01616563

ANYBODY
OUT THERE?

A COMEDY IN TWO ACTS

BY JOHN PATRICK

**DRAMATISTS
PLAY SERVICE
INC.**

ANYBODY OUT THERE?
Copyright © 1972, John Patrick
Copyright © 1971, John Patrick
as an unpublished dramatic composition

All Rights Reserved

CAUTION: Professionals and amateurs are hereby warned that performance of ANYBODY OUT THERE? is subject to a royalty. It is fully protected under the copyright laws of the United States of America, and of all countries covered by the International Copyright Union (including the Dominion of Canada and the rest of the British Commonwealth), and of all countries covered by the Pan-American Copyright Convention, the Universal Copyright Convention, the Berne Convention, and of all countries with which the United States has reciprocal copyright relations. All rights, including professional/amateur stage rights, motion picture, recitation, lecturing, public reading, radio broadcasting, television, video or sound recording, all other forms of mechanical or electronic reproduction, such as CD-ROM, CD-I, information storage and retrieval systems and photocopying, and the rights of translation into foreign languages, are strictly reserved. Particular emphasis is placed upon the matter of readings, permission for which must be secured from the Author's agent in writing.

The amateur performance rights in ANYBODY OUT THERE? are controlled exclusively by the DRAMATISTS PLAY SERVICE, INC., 440 Park Avenue South, New York, N.Y. 10016. No non-professional performance of the Play may be given without obtaining in advance the written permission of the DRAMATISTS PLAY SERVICE, INC., and paying the requisite fee.

Inquiries concerning all other rights should be addressed to the author c/o Dramatists Play Service, Inc., 440 Park Avenue South, New York, N.Y., 10016.

SPECIAL NOTE
Anyone receiving permission to produce ANYBODY OUT THERE? is required to give credit to the Author as sole and exclusive Author of the Play on the title page of all programs distributed in connection with performances of the Play and in all instances in which the title of the Play appears for purposes of advertising, publicizing or otherwise exploiting the Play and/or a production thereof. The name of the Author must appear on a separate line, in which no other name appears, immediately beneath the title and in size of type equal to 50% of the largest, most prominent letter used for the title of the Play. No person, firm or entity may receive credit larger or more prominent than that accorded the Author.

AUTHOR'S NOTE

There was insufficient time to stage this play (one of the playwright's five new plays) in community theatre and meet the printer's deadline for the year. There are, therefore, the usual flaws of staging inherent in any new play. The author begs your indulgence and relies on the discretion and taste of the director to alter and amend what would otherwise have been duly noted and corrected.

The sets should be spare to facilitate a quick change and the play itself, which borders on farce, played with exuberance and good will.

JOHN PATRICK

CAST

ACT I

ACT II

ANYBODY OUT THERE?

ACT I

SCENE 1

TIME: *The present. Morning.*

PLACE: *The bedroom of Oliver Pankey in a second-rate rooming house. It is a rather cramped room with a sofa that folds into a bed thereby making it impossible to open the door. Beside the sofa is an end table with lamp, radio, hot plate and alarm clock. There is one chair. A window, D. R., looks into an air shaft. There are two doors R.— one is a closet and the other leads into a bathroom.*

AT RISE: *Oliver, in a conservative nightshirt, is asleep with an eye mask on. The alarm rings. He sits up and feels about wildly before realizing he has on his sleeping mask. He shuts off the alarm. Oliver is a young man in his twenties, tense and tentative, not unattractive in a youthful, wholesome way. He puts on his glasses and looks at the alarm clock. He gets out of bed and steps to the window. He takes several deep breaths, exhaling them into the room. He then takes several vitamin pills, swallowing them with a glass of water beside the bed. Following this he puts a tea kettle on the hot plate and turns it on. He tunes in music on his small table radio. Having finished these diurnal duties, he picks up his pants and goes into his bathroom. Towels have been spread on the floor leading to the bathroom. The Announcer's voice fades in on the radio as he disappears.*

ANNOUNCER. "Good morning friends, this is Captain Penguin, bringing you the Happiness Hour again. Wake up, you sleepy-heads. It's a g-l-o-r-i-o-u-s day. Birds are singing, sun beams are dancing, happy flowers are smiling and there's a half-hour delay

5

on the West Side Parkway. It's a beautiful day so welcome it with a happy heart. Say good morning to a stranger. All you good folks out there in television, shout 'Good morning,' all of you— together. Let's hear it." (*He pauses. In the silence we hear a shout from the air shaft.*)

VOICE. Shut off that damn radio!

ANNOUNCER. (*Over the radio.*) "I didn't hear you, folks. Once more."

VOICE. You-stupid-on-the-third-floor. I'm trying to sleep. Turn off that blabber-box.

ANNOUNCER. "Oh, you can do better than that." (*There is a silence and then the crash of a bottle breaking the window.*) "That's better. And now let's all sing Welcome to a Lovely Day."

OLIVER. (*Enters, now wearing just his pants. He turns off the set and calls cautiously out the window.*) Hey—you broke my window!

VOICE. (*Offstage.*) Next time I'll come down there and break your head.

OLIVER. If I knew who you were, I'd report you. (*For an answer, another Coke bottle comes hurtling through the window.*) Well, you don't have to be unpleasant about it. (*As he starts to pick up the glass, there is a knock on the door.*) Wait a minute. (*He folds up the sofa bed so then he can open the door. His landlady, Sophie Goggan, enters. She is a humorless, austere woman whose head seems to sit on her shoulders devoid of a neck.*) Oh, good morning, Miss Goggan.

SOPHIE. I happened to be in the hall. I heard glass breaking.

OLIVER. Someone threw a bottle through the window.

SOPHIE. Why?

OLIVER. I had my radio on. The Happiness Hour.

SOPHIE. You must have had it on too loud.

OLIVER. I was gargling.

SOPHIE. Then you'll have to pay for the damage.

OLIVER. But I didn't break it.

SOPHIE. If you provoke the neighbors, you're responsible. (*Looks at his night table.*) Ah ha! (*Goes over to the hot plate.*) Cooking in your room!

OLIVER. It's just hot water for tea.

6

SOPHIE. That's cooking as far as I'm concerned. (*Pulls plug out.*) Stinks up my whole building.

OLIVER. Tea doesn't stink, Miss Goggan. You can hardly smell it at all. Almost.

SOPHIE. Rules are rules. (*Takes hot plate by wire.*) I'll just have to confiscate this. You can have it back when you leave. And that might be very soon if you go on breaking rules.

OLIVER. I wouldn't have heated the kettle except the water in the tap isn't hot enough.

SOPHIE. So you're dissatisfied here?

OLIVER. Oh, no. I'm very happy here, Miss Goggan. It's a beautiful room. It has an air shaft and everything.

SOPHIE. (*Looks down at floor.*) What are you standing on!

OLIVER. My feet.

SOPHIE. You're standing on my bath towels.

OLIVER. Oh, that. I just put them down to walk on a few minutes before I put my shoes on.

SOPHIE. You walk on my towels!

OLIVER. Well, you see, you can catch athlete's foot if you're not careful.

SOPHIE. Are you insinuating that my floors have germs?

OLIVER. Well, I don't know who had this room before, and I'm just being careful.

SOPHIE. I'll tell you who had this room before. A charming, refined old lady of ninety-two and she didn't have athlete's foot.

OLIVER. (*Quickly picks up towels.*) In that case, I don't have to be careful.

SOPHIE. She loved this room. Paid her rent promptly and never complained. I rue the day she left here.

OLIVER. If she loved it so much, why'd she give it up? Why didn't you keep her.

SOPHIE. She *died*, that's why. We could hardly keep her after that.

OLIVER. She died *here*? In this room?

SOPHIE. You needn't worry. We had all the furniture fumigated.

OLIVER. She died—in *my* bed?

SOPHIE. You weren't in it—what difference does it make.

OLIVER. Well, it's just that no one's ever died in my bed before.

SOPHIE. How do you know? You don't throw a bed away simply because someone's died in it.

OLIVER. I know. But I'm not going to be happy in my bed after this.

SOPHIE. Then sleep on the floor and catch germs. Whatever you want. Well, I can't stand here all day listening to you complaining about a poor old soul dying here.

OLIVER. I wasn't complaining, Miss Goggan. After all, I have to die someday too.

SOPHIE. Well, please don't do it here. (*Picks up bottles from floor.*) I'll just take this bottle. There is a two-cent deposit on it. (*She goes out. Oliver turns his radio back on—cautiously this time. Again the voice of the announcer is heard, as Oliver returns to the bathroom.*)

ANNOUNCER. "And now our Glad Girl, Gloria Sunshine, will recite a poem dedicated to the Garden Club of Upper Monclair. Gloria—" (*The voice of the Sunshine Girl is heard.*)

GLORIA. "To a Rose." (*Reads.*)

> "They say a rose by any other name
> Would be the same
> Even as you and I.
> But did you know
> A rose can cry?
> It has a heart
> It has a brain
> To cut it causes cruel pain
> A rose can hurt—
> The pain can linger.
> Just like cutting off your finger
> And so before you cut another
> Tell me—would you cut your mother?"

ANNOUNCER. "Beautiful, Gloria! Just beautiful. Now for further commuter news. A station wagon full of Dominican nuns has overturned on the Throg's Neck Bridge causing traffic to be re-routed through the Jewish Cemetery. Since this is a one-way entrance there is a considerable delay." (*During a pause, there is a knock on the door.*) "Anyone contemplating a funeral today would be wise to postpone it." (*Oliver comes out and opens his door. A girl about his own age, Millie Milhaus, enters. She is rather attractive in an unobtrusive way, and seems a little uneasy to have interrupted.*)

OLIVER. Oh, hi, Millie. Am I late?

MILLIE. No—I'm early. I wanted to talk to you.

OLIVER. Well, we better keep the door ajar. You know Miss Goggan's rules.

MILLIE. I know. I wonder if I did the right thing in suggesting you rent a room here.

OLIVER. Did you know an old lady died in my bed?

MILLIE. When?

OLIVER. Once. I don't know when.

MILLIE. Oliver, can I talk to you? Serious?

OLIVER. Can't we talk on the subway?

MILLIE. That's what I wanted to talk about. I don't think I should go to work with you anymore on the subway.

OLIVER. You want to take the bus?

MILLIE. Oliver—I want to get married.

OLIVER. I know. To me.

MILLIE. You don't understand.

OLIVER. Yes I do. You don't want to wait a year. And I don't blame you. So I'm going to ask Mister Henderson this morning for a raise. I promise you, we won't have to wait for my mother to go on Social Security.

MILLIE. Oliver—listen. You don't understand. I'm going to marry someone else.

OLIVER. (Stares at her.) I don't understand.

MILLIE. I just said that.

OLIVER. You mean you want to marry someone besides me?

MILLIE. In a way—yes.

OLIVER. But you can't marry someone else when you're engaged to me.

MILLIE. I know. That's why I thought I ought to break our engagement.

OLIVER. But what have I done?

MILLIE. Nothing. And that's why I fell in love with Herbie. He does things.

OLIVER. Herbie? At the bank.

MILLIE. He's going places, Oliver. He's a fighter.

OLIVER. He's a phony.

MILLIE. You're always afraid of trouble, Oliver. And that's the trouble.

OLIVER. Well, if it's trouble you want, Herbie Henderson will give you plenty, believe me, all right, all right.

9

MILLIE. He stands up for his rights. You don't. You let subway guards push you. You don't even talk back to waiters when they're rude.

OLIVER. I don't leave a tip.

MILLIE. And you even eat things you didn't order.

OLIVER. Sometimes they're better.

MILLIE. Herbie makes me feel protected.

OLIVER. You need protection from a waiter?

MILLIE. And another thing. You haven't ever tried to kiss me since we got engaged.

OLIVER. There was a good reason.

MILLIE. There are no good reasons for not kissing.

OLIVER. I didn't want to defile you.

MILLIE. What does that mean?

OLIVER. All right. I'll tell you the truth then. I think I have a venereal disease.

MILLIE. A what!

OLIVER. Maybe I should have said social disease. But it doesn't make it any better.

MILLIE. But you—of all people! You couldn't!

OLIVER. It was an emergency.

MILLIE. An emergency!

OLIVER. Oh, I wasn't unfaithful to you.

MILLIE. If you got what you said you got, you couldn't have got it without being social.

OLIVER. Oh, yes, you can. Two weeks ago I had to use a subway rest room in a hurry. I was very careful. I even walked on my heels. But I caught something.

MILLIE. In your heels?

OLIVER. From the seat. I've been itching ever since. Tuesday I went to a doctor for a blood test.

MILLIE. What did he say.

OLIVER. I get a report today.

MILLIE. Who's the doctor?

OLIVER. I picked him out of the *Yellow Pages*. I gave a wrong address and I said my name was John Doe. I wish I'd said it was Herbie Henderson.

MILLIE. Your blood test won't change things, Oliver. (*Takes off ring.*) I think you'll want our engagement ring back.

10

OLIVER. *I* can't wear it. Look, Millie, don't be impulsive. Wait. I'll ask for a raise. *Today.* Before lunch.

MILLIE. *(Shakes her head.)* Someone else will come along to make you happy, Oliver.

OLIVER. I'd rather be miserable with you. Look—can't you wait until tomorrow?

MILLIE. Why tomorrow?

OLIVER. Today's my birthday. I hate to feel sorry I'm born on my birthday.

MILLIE. All right, Oliver. And don't you mention at the bank that I've broken our engagement. It would make me look frivolous.

OLIVER. And don't you mention my social disease. That would make me look frivolous too.

MILLIE. I'm sorry, Oliver, I really am. Because you always smell so clean.

OLIVER. I'm neat.

MILLIE. *(Goes to the door.)* I'll see you at the bank. *(Opens door.)* I hope your blood turns out all right. *(She goes out. Oliver looks at the ring in his hand and sighs. He tries to make it sparkle but nothing sparkles for Oliver today. He puts it on the table and returns to the bathroom. After a moment, a disreputable-looking young man enters stealthily and closes the door behind him. He takes Oliver's suitcase out of the closet and opens it on the sofa. He proceeds to put all of Oliver's suits into it. Having cleaned out the closet, he next takes the radio and packs that. Oliver comes out of the bathroom, an electric shaver in hand. He halts in alarm. The thief quickly draws a knife.)*

OLIVER. What are you doing in my room?

THIEF. What does it look like?

OLIVER. Where is my radio? *(Sees open suitcase.)* What are you doing with my clothes?

THIEF. I'm taking them to the cleaners.

OLIVER. No. You're taking *me* to the cleaners. You're a thief.

THIEF. You want to start calling names? All right—I'll start calling you "corpse."

OLIVER. *(Backs up.)* Are you going to kill me? It's my birthday.

THIEF. *(Holds out his hand.)* Let's have that shaver.

OLIVER. *(Oliver hands it over quickly.)* It's really not any good.

THIEF. I got a light beard.

OLIVER. Couldn't I just finish shaving? I'm late for work.

THIEF. What time is it?

OLIVER. (*Looks at his wrist watch.*) Eight ten.

THIEF. Good. Gimme your watch.

OLIVER. Look—take the alarm clock. I need my watch.

THIEF. (*Jabs the knife at Oliver.*) Don't make me mad.

OLIVER. (*Quickly hands him the watch.*) I was just trying to be helpful. It isn't waterproof.

THIEF. (*Examines watch.*) Where'd you ever find a cheap watch like this?

OLIVER. Well, it isn't easy.

THIEF. A cloth strap, too!

OLIVER. It's washable.

THIEF. You ought to be ashamed of yourself wearing a cheap watch like this.

OLIVER. If you wear your shirt sleeves long, your cuffs will cover it.

THIEF. What size shirt do you wear?

OLIVER. Fifteen and a half.

THIEF. Good. That's my size. Gimme your shirts.

OLIVER. (*Quickly opens table drawer and takes out a couple of shirts.*) Could I keep one to go to work in?

THIEF. (*Takes shirts.*) You only got two shirts!

OLIVER. Three. One's in the laundry.

THIEF. (*Looks at shirts.*) Man—have you got lousy taste.

OLIVER. They're drip-dry, if you're in a hurry, and in your profession, I'll bet that's important.

THIEF. I hate dealing with cheap people.

OLIVER. I'm not cheap, really. I'm saving up to get married.

THIEF. You're breaking my heart.

OLIVER. Honest. (*Shows him engagement ring.*) Here's my engagement ring.

THIEF. Now we're in business. Gimme. (*Holds out his hand.*)

OLIVER. I can't. There're two more installments due.

THIEF. I'll pay 'em. (*Takes ring.*)

OLIVER. But you can't use it!

THIEF. How do you know. I got me a chick, too.

OLIVER. I'm sure she wouldn't want to wear a stolen engagement ring. It starts a marriage off wrong.

THIEF. I wouldn't insult her with a cheap ring like this. I wouldn't put this ring in a pig's nose.

12

OLIVER. I'm sure the lady isn't that. (*Adds quickly.*) Sir.
THIEF. (*Shakes head sadly.*) Half the stuff I get nowadays is pure junk.
OLIVER. Things are bad all over.
THIEF. I probably won't get two bucks for this ring.
OLIVER. (*Quickly takes out his wallet.*) I'll give you twenty.
THIEF. How much you got there? (*Holds out his hand.*)
OLIVER. (*Quickly tries to put wallet back.*) I was going to give you a check.
THIEF. Let's have it!
OLIVER. (*Stands over wallet.*) Please! I drew that money out to send my mother. A hundred and thirty six fifty. She needs it.
THIEF. You think I haven't got a mother?
OLIVER. She's not well. She's fifty nine and arthritic.
THIEF. Mine's sixty four and alcoholic. I need it more than you.
OLIVER. Well, can I at least keep the empty wallet?
THIEF. I'll mail you my old one. Now—take off your pants.
OLIVER. What are you going to do!
THIEF. Guess.
OLIVER. You're going to castrate me!
THIEF. Don't worry, I'm going to leave you something. I just want them pants. They match this coat.
OLIVER. (*Taking off his pants.*) How am I going to get to work?
THIEF. I'll give you a lift.
OLIVER. I'll be fired.
THIEF. Where do you work?
OLIVER. At a bank. The Friendly Dime and Dollar.
THIEF. You a big shot?
OLIVER. Oh, no. I'm just a teller. It's only a branch office. There're just three of us.
THIEF. Where's it at.
OLIVER. Prospect and Freeway.
THIEF. I'll be seein' you. (*Oliver now stands in his shorts.*) Now, turn around.
OLIVER. Why?
THIEF. Do like I say.
OLIVER. (*Trembles.*) You going to stab me in the back?
THIEF. Put your hands behind you.
OLIVER. Good. I was worried.

THIEF. (*Ties his hands behind him.*) You're pretty baggy-assed for your age.
OLIVER. I know. It runs in the family.
THIEF. (*Pushes him down on the sofa.*) Now listen. I'm goin'. But if I hear a yell out of you before I'm out of this building, I'll come back and slice you into Sukiyaki.
OLIVER. You're just going to walk out and leave me like this?
THIEF. You want me to kiss you?
OLIVER. No. I just want you to leave me a dime so I can phone. I'll have to tell the bank I'll be late.
THIEF. I'll stop by and explain. (*Takes suitcase to the door.*) This has hardly been worth my time. (*He goes out. Oliver sits silently on the sofa a minute.*)
OLIVER. This day hasn't started off right!

CURTAIN

ACT I

Scene 2

Time: *A couple of hours later.*
Place: *The Dime and Dollar Bank.*
At Rise: *There is a plain counter u. with two teller windows. Millie is seen behind one of the windows checking figures. There is no one at Oliver's window.*
Off to one side there is a floor desk with a brass sign saying: "Herbert Henderson, Mgr." "Herbie" is the sort of executive who brushes imaginary crumbs off his vest. After a moment, he looks up in annoyance.

HERBIE. Millie?
MILLIE. Yes, Sweetheart—I mean—Yes, Mr. Henderson?
HERBIE. Have you any idea what could have happened to Oliver?
MILLIE. I didn't want to mention it, Herbie, but I'm worried sick.
HERBIE. Because he's late?
MILLIE. Two hours!
HERBIE. I don't know why I tolerate that mousey little man. It's a credit to my good nature.

14

MILLIE. Herbie—I'm afraid he's committed suicide.

HERBIE. (*Rises quickly.*) Suicide! Oh, my God. What a terrible thing for the bank! (*Crosses to Millie.*) Why would he do a thing like that to us?

MILLIE. Well, he was awfully depressed when I left him this morning.

HERBIE. Did he have a gun?

MILLIE. He's afraid of guns.

HERBIE. Do you think he might have jumped out his window?

MILLIE. He's afraid of heights.

HERBIE. Could he have cut his wrists?

MILLIE. Not with an electric razor.

HERBIE. Would he drown himself in the tub?

MILLIE. Not easily. He just has a shower.

HERBIE. Well, if he doesn't show up in ten minutes, we better start checking our books out in a hurry.

MILLIE. Oh, he wouldn't have stolen anything from the bank. He'd be afraid to.

HERBIE. If Oliver hasn't stolen anything from the bank, why would he want to commit suicide?

MILLIE. A broken heart. Oh, Herbie, this is terrible.

HERBIE. It certainly is. Depositors lose confidence when bank tellers commit suicide. They think we're both unstable.

MILLIE. It could all be my fault, Herbie.

HERBIE. Why?

MILLIE. I told him about us this morning.

HERBIE. You what!

MILLIE. I told him we were going to be married.

HERBIE. (*Shouts.*) You idiot! Have you lost your mind? What if my wife hears about this?

MILLIE. (*Aghast.*) You've got a wife?

HERBIE. (*Recovers quickly.*) Now, sweetheart, I didn't mention it before because I didn't want to upset you, darling. You see, she's in an institution.

MILLIE. (*Wails.*) You've got a wife! Alive.

HERBIE. Now, Millie, she's like a stranger to me. A total stranger.

MILLIE. You never told me when we got engaged that you were married.

HERBIE. The subject never came up. Now control yourself. You mustn't be emotional where money is entrusted.

15

MILLIE. You were emotional enough with me last week down in the safety vault.

HERBIE. The bank was closed. I have never been emotional during banking hours.

MILLIE. I trusted you. I thought if there was one place a girl could be safe, it would be the safety vault.

HERBIE. Stop crying! You're getting the money wet.

MILLIE. Do you have any children?

HERBIE. My wife is a Catholic.

MILLIE. Well, she can't be a nun. How many children?

HERBIE. A few.

MILLIE. How few?

HERBIE. Seven.

MILLIE. (*Shrieks.*) SEVEN!

HERBIE. (*Jumps as if shot.*) Seven isn't a lot.

MILLIE. It's a lot for a stranger.

HERBIE. Actually, it's only six and a half.

MILLIE. You've got a midget?

HERBIE. My wife is four months pregnant.

MILLIE. In an institution?

HERBIE. Now, Millie, if you're going to cry, I'll have to ask you to go down to the safety vault.

MILLIE. You'll never get me in that safety vault again. You have no respect for money.

HERBIE. Wipe your nose. Look happy. Here comes someone. (*He hurries back to his desk. Oliver enters. At first glance, he is unrecognizable. He has on a suit several times too large for him. His baggy pants are held up by a rope. He crosses to Herbie.*)

OLIVER. Good morning. I'm late.

MILLIE. Oliver! It's you!

HERBIE. Mister Pankey! What do you mean coming into the bank dressed like that?

OLIVER. My clothes were stolen. I had to borrow these from the janitor. He's obliging but obese.

MILLIE. We thought maybe you'd jumped out your window.

OLIVER. Naked? A thief took everything I had. (*Takes an alarm clock and a tooth brush out of his baggy pockets.*) This is all he left me. My entire estate consists of a toothbrush and an alarm clock.

MILLIE. Well, at least you're alive.

OLIVER. I'd have phoned but I didn't have a dime. I walked.
HERBIE. Well, get behind the counter before anyone sees you.
OLIVER. Could I talk to you a minute, first? It's very important.
(*To Millie.*) I'm going to keep my promise, Millie.
HERBIE. Make it quick.
OLIVER. Well, as you know I've been with the bank here for five years. Five loyal years.
HERBIE. Only five? Seems more like ten.
OLIVER. And I didn't start at a very big salary.
HERBIE. Do you know what the average daily wage is in Mali?
OLIVER. Where's Mali?
HERBIE. Oliver, you owe it to the bank to keep up with current affairs. Mali is in Africa and they earn forty two cents a day. As a matter of fact their ambassador is one of our depositors.
OLIVER. He deposits forty two cents?
HERBIE. It's prestige that counts. What did you want?
OLIVER. Well; as you know, the dollar isn't worth as much now as it was five years ago. Even forty two cents isn't.
HERBIE. You can say that again.
OLIVER. I think once makes the point.
HERBIE. And just what is the point?
OLIVER. Well; living costs have gone up and we have to take a practical point of view, don't we?
HERBIE. We certainly do. And I'm glad to see you take that point of view. I was going to bring up the subject myself. Do you realize how much costs have gone up here at the bank? Paper clips have doubled.
OLIVER. I was speaking of my problems, sir.
HERBIE. They're one and the same, Oliver. What's bad for the bank is bad for the people.
OLIVER. What I wanted to point out, sir, was that my salary here is submarginal.
HERBIE. Not in Mali. And as you said, we've got to be practical. Do you consider yourself the kind of employee who would pitch in here and help?
OLIVER. Oh, yes. This bank is my home.
HERBIE. Then do you think we'd be unfair if we asked you to take a ten per cent cut in salary?
OLIVER. Ten per cent!
HERBIE. In Mali that would only be four cents a day.

17

OLIVER. Could we make it four cents a day here, then?

HERBIE. Ah, but costs here have gone up fifty per cent. Would you feel better to make it twenty per cent?

OLIVER. No-no! Ten per cent is fine.

HERBIE. You're happy at that figure?

OLIVER. Oh, yes, sir. I'm very happy.

HERBIE. You're sure?

OLIVER. Positive.

HERBIE. Then we've nothing more to discuss, have we, Oliver?

OLIVER. No, sir.

HERBIE. Except for one thing. Would you pay a man for not working?

OLIVER. No, sir.

HERBIE. Good. Then we'll deduct for the two hours you're late this morning. Now, anything else?

OLIVER. Yes, sir. Could I arrange with the bank for a loan?

HERBIE. Interest rates have gone up, you know.

OLIVER. Since yesterday?

HERBIE. It's a tight market. How much of a loan did you want?

OLIVER. A hundred and thirty six dollars and fifty eight cents. My mother's not on Social Security yet.

HERBIE. What's the eight cents for?

OLIVER. Postage.

HERBIE. What do you do with all your money, Oliver?

OLIVER. Lately I have it stolen.

HERBIE. What can you offer as security?

OLIVER. My salary here.

HERBIE. It's just been cut ten per cent.

OLIVER. I have a life insurance policy and you could sell my body to a medical school.

HERBIE. They're not accepting white bodies anymore. Discrimination, you know.

OLIVER. It's only one hundred and thirty six dollars and fifty eight cents.

HERBIE. Only! Do you realize that ten years ago that much would have been worth over a thousand dollars?

OLIVER. Golly. That means ten years from now, I'll really have borrowed two thousand dollars.

HERBIE. Maybe more.

OLIVER. Then the ten per cent cut I've just taken will really be twenty per cent, won't it?

HERBIE. But you'll be paying less taxes.

OLIVER. Then shouldn't we make my cut five per cent now so that it'll be ten per cent later?

HERBIE. You're not thinking like a bank, Oliver. You've got to remember also that your life insurance policy will only be worth half of what it is today.

OLIVER. Maybe it would pay me to die now.

HERBIE. You'd be ahead.

OLIVER. If you could just make it one hundred and thirty six dollars and fifty cents, I'll raise the eight cents postage.

HERBIE. Bring in your policy and I'll see. We appreciate loyalty here. And, of course, honesty, too. Your bank is your friend.

OLIVER. Oh, thank you very much. (*Pumps his hand gratefully.*) And thank you for the cut, too.

HERBIE. Anytime. Now, you'd better get to work.

OLIVER. Could I go to the men's room first? I don't feel well, sir.

HERBIE. Don't take too long. Time is money. (*Looks up from his desk as Oliver stands there.*) Well, what is it now?

OLIVER. Could I have the key, please?

HERBIE. (*Hands him key.*) Ten more years, Oliver, and you'll be entitled to your own key.

OLIVER. Yes, sir. Only ten years. That'll be a lot of water under the bridge, won't it? (*He goes out. Millie leans over the counter to address Herbie.*)

MILLIE. Seven children!

HERBIE. Stop dwelling on personal problems. You'll make a mistake in the payroll.

MILLIE. I've already made one. In the safety vault. How old are they?

HERBIE. The oldest boy is twenty one.

MILLIE. Twenty one! I'm only twenty. I'll have a son older than I am.

HERBIE. He's old enough to understand.

MILLIE. He's old enough to rape me.

HERBIE. That's hardly likely. He's in the army.

MILLIE. That's worse. He'll be coming back with experience.

HERBIE. Millie, a bank is no place to discuss sex. It's not the kind of interest we encourage. (*Looks off.*) Be careful—there's a man

19

coming in. (*The thief who robbed Oliver enters and looks around. Herbie crosses to him.*) Good morning. Lovely day, isn't it?

THIEF. If you could find a place to park.

HERBIE. We expect to have our own parking lot just across the street just as soon as they tear the church down.

THIEF. Nice little bank you've got here. Very convenient.

HERBIE. Oh, yes, indeed. We're close to the highway, the parkway and the throughway. Nothing to hold you up.

THIEF. That's the kind of location I like.

HERBIE. How can I help you?

THIEF. You're doing fine. Only two of you here?

HERBIE. Three. But we're prepared to take care of all of your needs.

THIEF. That's good to know.

HERBIE. And just what can I do for you, sir?

THIEF. I was planning to do a little business with you.

HERBIE. Are you in this area?

THIEF. I'm moving in.

HERBIE. May I ask what your line is?

THIEF. Interstate commerce.

HERBIE. Must be demanding work.

THIEF. Keeps you on the run. Where's your third clerk?

HERBIE. He's down in the—er—safety vault.

THIEF. Where's that?

HERBIE. In the basement. Would you like to see it?

THIEF. I had that in mind.

HERBIE. If you'll just follow me please. (*Herbie starts off with the thief at his heels. A police officer enters from the front.*)

OFFICER. Hey—you! (*The thief and Herbie stop and turn toward the officer.*)

THIEF. Me?

OFFICER. That's right. (*Crosses to them.*) That your car double parked in front?

THIEF. I was coming right out.

OFFICER. Well, you got me blocked in. I ought to give you a ticket.

HERBIE. This gentlemen is a bank prospect, Officer.

OFFICER. He's still blocking traffic.

THIEF. (*To Herbie.*) I guess my business will have to wait. What time do you close?

HERBIE. Three. But don't worry. I'll wait for you.

THIEF. I'll be back. (*Goes out.*)

HERBIE. Important businessman. I can always tell.

OFFICER. Well, as long as I'm here, I might as well cash a check. It's poker night. (*Crosses to counter.*)

HERBIE. I do hope the gentleman comes back. (*Goes to his desk.*)

OFFICER. (*At counter.*) Anything wrong, Miss?

MILLIE. I've got a cold.

OFFICER. How'd you get it?

MILLIE. I was exposed to a nasty germ.

OFFICER. Lot of it going around. All last week, during the riots, I was out with a cold.

MILLIE. Was it bad?

OFFICER. Was it bad! Two of my buddies were shot in the butt.

MILLIE. Did you see a doctor?

OFFICER. No—but I saw a lot of television.

MILLIE. How would you like your money?

OFFICER. Tax free. (*Laughs at his own wit.*)

MILLIE. Fives all right?

OFFICER. Fives are fine. Tens are better. (*Pockets money.*) Don't pay to carry a lot of money. I been mugged twice. There wasn't a cop within two miles.

HERBIE. Thank heaven's there's nothing like that in this neighborhood.

OFFICER. Keep it like that. I got a wife and kids. (*Starts out and meets Sophie entering pushing a shopping cart filled with bags.*) Hi, Miss Goggan. Hear you had some trouble over your way.

SOPHIE. And where were you?

OFFICER. Right where I belong. Directing traffic. (*He goes out.*)

HERBIE. Good morning, Miss Goggan. (*Notices her shopping cart.*) Been to the supermarket?

SOPHIE. These aren't groceries I got here. It's money.

HERBIE. Those bags are all filled with money?

SOPHIE. Pennies are money, aren't they?

HERBIE. Those bags are all filled with pennies?

SOPHIE. I been saving pennies in tins and shoe boxes for over forty years. What with thieves breaking into my building, I collected 'em all, I decided they weren't safe lying around outside of a bank.

HERBIE. You must have a couple of thousand dollars in pennies saved there, Miss Goggan.

SOPHIE. Could be more. I don't know.

HERBIE. Haven't you counted them?

SOPHIE. Why should I count them? It's a bank's job to count money, isn't it?

HERBIE. Yes, indeed. You might say it's our favorite pastime.

SOPHIE. Do you have a machine to count it?

HERBIE. Oh, yes. It's washing it's hands right now but I'll see if it's ready. (*Turns to call.*) Oliver!

SOPHIE. You letting Oliver Pankey count my pennies?

HERBIE. It will give me great pleasure.

SOPHIE. How do I know I can trust him? He's so rattled, he could make a mistake.

HERBIE. I'll have him count them twice. (*Oliver appears.*) Well, you certainly took long enough.

OLIVER. My zipper stuck.

SOPHIE. My janitor wants his suit back by tonight, Mister Pankey. Pressed.

OLIVER. I'm buying a new suit after work.

SOPHIE. And just what are you going to use for money?

OLIVER. I'm negotiating a loan from the bank.

HERBIE. I can't understand how you let the thief take everything you had, Oliver.

OLIVER. He had a knife.

HERBIE. Why didn't you take it away from him?

OLIVER. I didn't want to die on my birthday.

HERBIE. Today's your birthday?

OLIVER. All day.

HERBIE. Well, I have a present for you. Miss Goggan has some pennies she wants counted. And I'm going to give you the privilege of counting them for her.

SOPHIE. Twice.

OLIVER. Those are all pennies?

HERBIE. Miss Goggan has been very thrifty.

SOPHIE. That represents forty years of saving pennies.

HERBIE. Now I have a date to have lunch with the president. So you can use my desk.

SOPHIE. The president?

HERBIE. Of the bank.

22

OLIVER. Sir, won't it look bad for depositors to come in and see me counting pennies?

HERBIE. On the contrary, it will set a good example.

SOPHIE. I'll just sit here and wait, if you don't mind.

HERBIE. I'm afraid this will take the rest of the day.

SOPHIE. I brought my knitting.

OLIVER. Mister Henderson, I have an important date with my doctor at one.

HERBIE. Then you'll just have to stay tonight until you've finished. (*To Sophie.*) Would you like some coffee while he's counting?

SOPHIE. Tea, if you don't mind.

HERBIE. I'll have it sent in. Now, if you'll excuse me, I have to meet the president. (*To Oliver.*) Oliver, we may play golf after lunch. If I'm not back by closing time, there is a businessman coming back for some bank business. He's in interstate commerce.

OLIVER. Yes, sir.

HERBIE. See that he gets everything that he wants.

OLIVER. Yes, sir.

HERBIE. I will hold you responsible.

OLIVER. Yes, sir.

HERBIE. Enjoy your knitting, Miss Goggan. Millie, keep an eye on things. Oliver, start counting. (*He goes out jauntily.*)

OLIVER. (*Reaches into first sack of pennies.*) One—two—three—four—five—six—seven. . . . . .

SOPHIE. See that you don't make a mistake.

OLIVER. I think I've already made one.

SOPHIE. Just now?

OLIVER. This morning. I think I should have let that thief kill me. (*Resumes counting.*) Eight—nine—ten—eleven—twelve. . . .

CURTAIN

ACT I

SCENE 3

TIME: *Lunch hour. Same day.*
PLACE: *Doctor's office.*
AT RISE: *Anita Wrenn sits at her receptionist's desk*

polishing her nails. She is a brassy, pert, pretty miniature martinet. (Or, if you choose to cast her so, she can be a fat slob but it will betray a perverted taste.)
There is a bench against the upper wall. There is a door frame separating the waiting room from the doctor's office.
Doctor Dickey stands in his office looking at his tongue in a wall mirror. He looks more like a golf Pro. If you can't find a healthy looking doctor, any will do in an emergency.
The office consists of a desk and a cabinet file—facilitating a quick scene change.
Before the lights come up, Oliver's voice can be heard again as he counts: "—three thousand, two hundred and fifty one, three thousand, two hundred and fifty two, three thousand, two hundred and fifty three—" etc.
A few moments after the lights come up, Oliver enters. The doctor returns to his desk to read Playboy.
Anita continues her preoccupation with her nails. Oliver coughs.

ANITA. You shouldn't smoke so much.
OLIVER. I don't smoke at all. Is the doctor in?
ANITA. What did you want?
OLIVER. I wanted to see him.
ANITA. Do you have an appointment?
OLIVER. Naturally.
ANITA. Not necessarily. Name?
OLIVER. Doe.
ANITA. Will you spell it, please. Doctor's orders.
OLIVER. "D" as in "diarrhea." "O" as in ovary and "E" as in "enema."
ANITA. Is "Doe" your first or last name?
OLIVER. It could hardly be first. Otherwise, I'd be dodo.
ANITA. (*Looks at him.*) Could be. First name, please?
OLIVER. John. (*Spells it.*) J-o-h-n. "J" as in "Jabberwocky," "O" as in "Oberammergau," "H" as in "heliotropism" and "N" as in "nuts."
ANITA. Are you Blue Cross, Blue Shield, Medicare, Pension or Relief?

24

OLIVER. Miss, we went through that when I was here before.
ANITA. You've been here before?
OLIVER. Last week.
ANITA. That was another girl. Now. Preoperative, postoperative, preliminary or exploratory?
OLIVER. I had a blood test. All I want to know is the results.
ANITA. Did we notify you?
OLIVER. I said I'd come back.
ANITA. Today?
OLIVER. Ten minutes ago. Miss, I work at a bank. I've got to be back. Will you kindly tell the doctor that I'm here.
ANITA. Have a seat, please. (*She picks up a book to read.*)
OLIVER. Miss, aren't you going to let the doctor know I'm here?
ANITA. *I* know you're here. Doctor will ring when he's ready to see patients.
OLIVER. But I had an appointment for one o'clock!
ANITA. You had an appointment to *be* here at one o'clock. That doesn't mean that the doctor *sees* you at one o'clock. You will notice that this is called a waiting room, Mister Doe. Not a launching pad.
OLIVER. Miss, I've had a bad day. PLEASE tell the doctor I'm here.
ANITA. (*Rises.*) Very well. Patients have no consideration for the doctor. (*Goes into Doctor's office. The doctor looks up.*)
DOCTOR. What's on your mind, doll?
ANITA. Another one of those impatient patients.
DOCTOR. Young, old, black, white, male, or female?
ANITA. In between.
DOCTOR. What name?
ANITA. John Doe.
DOCTOR. Doesn't sound familiar. What does he look like?
ANITA. One of the Seven Dwarfs.
DOCTOR. What does he want?
ANITA. Wants to know the results of a blood test you gave him.
DOCTOR. Have we got his test back?
ANITA. Should have. Shall I send him in?
DOCTOR. How long has he been waiting?
ANITA. Just came in.
DOCTOR. Oh, then we can't possibly see him right away. Sets a

25

bad example. Have him wait half an hour. (*Picks up* Playboy *again.*)

ANITA. Ring when you're ready.

DOCTOR. Bring in his report when I see him.

ANITA. (*Points to his files.*) Should be in your files. (*Goes to door.*) If it isn't under "D" for "Doe," it's under "B" for "blood." I forget which.

DOCTOR. You're a gorgeous chick, Anita, but a lousy file clerk, sweetie. When I looked for "sacroiliac" under "S," I found a sandwich.

ANITA. Sorry. Next time I'll file my lunch under "L." (*Goes out. She addresses Oliver.*) Doctor's in conference. He'll see you as soon as he's free.

OLIVER. How long will that be?

ANITA. I'm a receptionist, not an astrologer, Mister Doe. (*Picks up a book to read.*)

OLIVER. Did you tell the doctor that my appointment was for one o'clock and that I was here on time?

ANITA. Would you like to make an appointment for another day, Mister Doe?

OLIVER. No—no! I want to know what my blood test showed. Today.

ANITA. You'll find magazines on the table there—*Forbes, Fortune* and *Field and Stream.*

OLIVER. I read them last time.

ANITA. Well, there's a *Ladies' Home Journal* there if you're interested.

OLIVER. I know. Only it's a year old.

ANITA. Patients come here to complain about their illnesses, Mister Doe—not our magazines.

OLIVER. It was just a comment. (*He retreats behind his newspaper. Bill McSwain, a healthy extrovert, enters in a cloud of confidence.*)

BILL. Hi, there—beautiful.

ANITA. Oh, hello, Mister McSwain.

BILL. Doctor in?

ANITA. I'm sure he's in for you, Mister McSwain.

BILL. Tell him I want to see him right away. I have a golf date and I don't want to be late.

ANITA. Right away. (*She goes into the doctor's office. The*

26

doctor looks up from his magazine.) Doctor, Mister McSwain just dropped in. Wants to see you right away.
DOCTOR. Mac? Sure—send him right in.
ANITA. Yes, doctor.
DOCTOR. Wait a minute—get me that John Doe report out of the files. (*Anita goes to the doctor's files. As she searches, Oliver addresses McSwain.*)
OLIVER. Excuse me, but do you have an appointment?
BILL. Why?
OLIVER. Well, I have. One o'clock.
BILL. What about it?
OLIVER. Well, I have an appointment and I was here before you.
BILL. Congratulations.
OLIVER. So I'm next.
BILL. And who says I don't have an appointment?
OLIVER. Well, do you?
BILL. Look, fella— (*Shows him a badge.*) I'm with the F.B.I. For all you know, I'm here on official business.
OLIVER. Well, are you?
BILL. That's top secret, pal.
OLIVER. Well, I'll just ask the nurse, then.
BILL. (*Pushes his jaw into Oliver's face.*) What have we got here? A radical? You look like a suspicious character to me.
OLIVER. (*Sits down—defeated.*) I just thought you'd like to know I was here, first.
BILL. I'll see that that gets on your file.
OLIVER. Thank you. (*Anita puts Oliver's file on the doctor's desk and then opens the door.*)
ANITA. Doctor will see you now. (*Oliver jumps to his feet.*) Not you. (*To McSwain.*) You. (*Oliver sits down as McSwain goes into the doctor's office. Anita picks up her book again.*)
DOCTOR. Hi, Mac. This is a pleasant surprise.
BILL. Happened to be in the building. (*They shake hands.*)
DOCTOR. Glad you dropped in. Sit down.
BILL. (*Sits down beside desk and puts his feet up.*) How you been, Doc?
DOCTOR. I don't know. I got this pain in my back—my throat's sore—I can't sleep. I wake up tired. I'm not eating well. I'm short tempered and jittery. What do you suppose it is?
BILL. Filed your income tax?

27

DOCTOR. I got two more days.

BILL. Get it over with—you'll pick up right away.

DOCTOR. Might as well. I've tried everything else. Never mind me, how have you been feeling?

BILL. Well, I don't know how to begin. (*He looks at the ceiling and hesitates. Outside the office, Oliver takes his alarm clock out of his pocket and puts it on the bench beside him. He points to it.*)

OLIVER. My appointment was for one. It's one fifteen and a half. (*He pulls his newspaper up in front of his face before Anita can answer.*)

DOCTOR. (*To McSwain.*) Anything wrong with you? Your stomach—your golf?

BILL. Well, I'm having a little trouble. That's why I thought I ought to see you.

DOCTOR. What are your symptoms?

BILL. I haven't got any. It's not me. I feel fine. It's my wife.

DOCTOR. What's wrong with her?

BILL. She's frigid.

DOCTOR. Lately or always.

BILL. Just since she's taken up Yogi. She sits on the damn floor in that damn lotus position—eyes closed—legs crossed—arms folded and—boy! Try to get her untied.

DOCTOR. Can you communicate with her?

BILL. Not on that level.

DOCTOR. How long does she stay in that position?

BILL. I don't know. I'm fast asleep.

DOCTOR. I think you've got a problem.

BILL. She goes to this damn Hindu guru—a kind of dirty Santa Claus in a night gown. He tells her to put earthly things out of her mind. I don't think he bathes. He smells like a dill pickle.

DOCTOR. Have you tried reasoning with her?

BILL. She's a woman.

DOCTOR. But she must say something.

BILL. She does—"leave me alone—I'm meditating."

DOCTOR. Hmmm. Let's see what I can suggest. (*While the two men are thinking, Oliver lowers his newspaper and points to the alarm clock beside him.*)

OLIVER. It's one seventeen.

ANITA. I have a watch, Mister Doe.

OLIVER. I hope you look at it. (*He quickly disappears behind his paper again. In the office, McSwain leans confidentially toward the Doctor.)*

BILL. What's a good aphrodisiac?

DOCTOR. Why?

BILL. I thought maybe I could slip something into her yogurt.

DOCTOR. The best aphrodisiac I know of, is the opposite sex.

BILL. *I'm* that.

DOCTOR. I noticed.

BILL. Are oysters any good?

DOCTOR. Not in yogurt.

BILL. I mean—would they help arouse her?

DOCTOR. They're only good in a month with an "R" in it.

BILL. *(Counts.)* May—June—July—August . . . no—that's too long to wait.

DOCTOR. You've tried to inflame her?

BILL. I used everything but a blow torch.

DOCTOR. And she's still cold to you?

BILL. You could freeze ice-cream.

DOCTOR. Have you tried flowers?

BILL. Not as an aphrodisiac.

DOCTOR. Pills are not going to help.

BILL. What about cinnamon? I read someplace that a tablespoon full of cinnamon is a good aphrodisiac.

DOCTOR. Fallacy. It just makes you flatulent.

BILL. Well, that wouldn't arouse her.

DOCTOR. Besides, how would you get it down her?

BILL. Slip it into her Manhattan?

DOCTOR. Makes a lousy Manhattan.

BILL. Makes a lousy marriage.

DOCTOR. Why don't you get rid of her guru?

BILL. How!

DOCTOR. Slip him some cinnamon.

BILL. It would sure make him smell better. *(As they ponder the problem, Oliver, in the outer office lowers his newspaper.)*

OLIVER. It's one twenty.

ANITA. Is that supposed to mean something?

OLIVER. Just that we're both twenty minutes older. *(He hides behind his paper again. The doctor offers his guest a cigarette.)*

DOCTOR. Have a cigarette.

BILL. I've given that up, too.

DOCTOR. Wish I could.

BILL. Hey! How about pot?

DOCTOR. I wouldn't advise it. It affects the brain.

BILL. To hell with her brain—what does it do to the rest of her?

DOCTOR. There are too many bad side effects to pot.

BILL. There's too many bad side effects to sex, too. Lassitude, inertia—children.

DOCTOR. Besides, it's habit forming.

BILL. That's what I want.

DOCTOR. Have you tried any prefecunditory overtures?

BILL. You mean music?

DOCTOR. Like in nature. Have you ever watched animals mate?

BILL. We got gold fish. Watching them won't inflame you. She lays an egg and he swims over it.

DOCTOR. I mean red blooded animals. Stallions kick the mares, rams butt the ewes, and lions bite the females. It gets results.

BILL. Oh, come on, Doc. I can't bite her in the Lotus position and I damn well won't kick her while she's down.

DOCTOR. It was just an idea. (*As they concentrate, Oliver lowers his newspaper outside.*)

OLIVER. It's one twenty two.

ANITA. Would you like a gong?

OLIVER. No, thank you. I've set the alarm to ring at one thirty. (*He retreats behind his newspaper again. Inside, McSwain rises and paces nervously.*)

BILL. Doc—I did something very foolish this weekend. I've got a confession to make.

DOCTOR. What'd you do?

BILL. You won't laugh?

DOCTOR. I'm your friend.

BILL. (*Takes a small box out of his pocket.*) You know what I've got in this box?

DOCTOR. What?

BILL. Bees.

DOCTOR. What?

BILL. Bees. Dead bees. I spent the whole weekend trapping them.

DOCTOR. Why!

BILL. I have it on reliable authority, that the Navajo Indians use them for sex stimulation and it never fails.

DOCTOR. It's failed the Navajos.

30

BILL. Cleopatra ate them. It's part of history. I know it sounds crazy but I'm desperate.

DOCTOR. How are you going to make your wife get out of the lotus position to eat a dead bee?

BILL. I could bring home some chili—she wouldn't notice.

DOCTOR. You might kill her.

BILL. I may anyhow. But first, I'm going to find out if they work.

DOCTOR. How?

BILL. I'm going to be my own guinea-pig.

DOCTOR. You're going to test them on yourself?

BILL. That's why I thought I ought to be near a doctor.

DOCTOR. You're going to eat them here?

BILL. Right now.

DOCTOR. Raw?

BILL. You haven't got anything here I could eat them with, have you?

DOCTOR. I've got some cough medicine. You could wash them down with that but I don't think you'd like it.

BILL. It should be food.

DOCTOR. Wait a minute. Anita's got a sandwich in my files. (*Goes to files.*) She brings her lunch. (*Returns with sandwich.*) We'll borrow a sandwich from her. (*Opens wrapping.*) It looks like pastrami. Is that all right?

BILL. With bees, it doesn't matter.

DOCTOR. You want a knife to spread them?

BILL. One good thing about bees—you can sprinkle them. (*Puts top back on sandwich.*) Well, here goes.

DOCTOR. Look—if this works—do you think we ought to be in here together alone?

BILL. If I feel anything working, I'll take a taxi.

DOCTOR. Or a shower.

BILL. Want a bite? (*Extends sandwich.*)

DOCTOR. I'd rather bite my mother.

BILL. To Cleopatra. And the Navajos. (*Munches sandwich. The Doctor watches. He takes a second bite and chews slowly.*)

DOCTOR. What does it taste like?

BILL. Dead bees.

DOCTOR. Is it good pastrami?

BILL. I've had better. (*Takes another bite.*)

DOCTOR. How do you feel?

31

BILL. Foolish. How do I look?

DOCTOR. Foolish. I hope you know that the life expectancy of a Navajo is thirty five years.

BILL. With a frigid wife, what difference does it make?

DOCTOR. I better take your pulse. (*Takes Bill's wrist. Bill continues to chew.*)

BILL. If this works, we've got a gold mine.

DOCTOR. If it doesn't, we've got a lot of dead bees.

BILL. How's my pulse?

DOCTOR. Are you sure your heart's beating?

BILL. You've got your finger on my wrist band.

DOCTOR. I thought you felt cold blooded. (*Takes out stethoscope.*) I better check your breathing. (*He listens. Outside, Oliver's alarm clock goes off.*)

OLIVER. It's one thirty. (*Holds up alarm clock.*)

ANITA. You're slow. It's twenty to two.

OLIVER. What can you expect with trading stamps? (*As he sets his clock, the doctor in his office, straightens up.*)

BILL. Hear anything?

DOCTOR. I thought I heard an alarm clock. (*Glances down at his desk.*) Wait a minute! Stop eating!

BILL. Anything wrong?

DOCTOR. Where'd you get these bees?

BILL. Botanical Gardens. They were buzzing around the roses.

DOCTOR. Those aren't bees!

BILL. What are they?

DOCTOR. Japanese Beetles.

BILL. Beetles!

DOCTOR. Don't you know a bee when you see one?

BILL. I was born in Brooklyn.

DOCTOR. See what sex will drive you to!

BILL. (*Hurls sandwich into waste basket.*) I think I will kick her while she's down.

DOCTOR. Get rid of her guru. It's easier.

BILL. You want to know something, Doc?

DOCTOR. What?

BILL. I'll bet I'm the only man this side of Central Park South that's eaten a pastrami and beetle sandwich.

DOCTOR. I think I ought to take you out for a drink.

BILL. I could use it.

DOCTOR. I'll get my golf clubs and we'll take the day off.

BILL. My sex life may not improve but maybe my golf game will.

DOCTOR. Wait a minute. Damn! I've got a patient out there. Oh, well, I'll tell him to make another appointment. You're an emergency case.

BILL. I don't mind waiting. I feel a little queasy anyhow.

DOCTOR. It won't take a minute. It's just a blood test report.

BILL. Take your time. I have to digest my beetles.

DOCTOR. Have Anita send the patient in. (*McSwain starts for the door. Outside Oliver looks up.*)

OLIVER. Excuse me.

ANITA. Yes?

OLIVER. Could you tell me what time it is? (*Before Anita can answer, McSwain steps into the reception room.*)

BILL. Doc says send the next guy in.

ANITA. Thank you. (*To Oliver.*) Would you like to go in now?

OLIVER. If I haven't taken root. (*He rises and goes into the doctor's office. The doctor is engrossed in Oliver's report. Oliver clears his throat.*)

DOCTOR. Oh. Come in, Mister—er—er . . .

OLIVER. Doe. John Doe.

DOCTOR. Yes—yes. Sit down. I was just studying your report. (*Oliver sits beside the desk. The doctor continues to read the report, clucking ominously as he turns the pages. He mumbles "Ah ha!" and frowns. Oliver grows increasingly nervous.*)

OLIVER. Sir?

DOCTOR. (*Glances up.*) Yes?

OLIVER. You've got some dead beetles on your desk.

DOCTOR. Help yourself. I mean—brush them aside. (*He goes back to the report, pausing to mutter "tch—tch" occasionally. Oliver's hands begin to shake. Finally, the doctor looks up at him and stares in silence.*) Are you married, Mister Doe?

OLIVER. I was sort of planning.

DOCTOR. I would strongly advise against it.

OLIVER. You mean . . . I've got something?

DOCTOR. It's a case like yours that makes a doctor wish he were a dentist.

OLIVER. What do you mean?

DOCTOR. A physician has to look into a man's soul. A dentist only has to look into his mouth.

33

OLIVER. What are you trying to tell me—that I've got the Big "S"?

DOCTOR. Shall I tell you the truth?

OLIVER. I'd hate to think I've waited an hour to be lied to.

DOCTOR. The naked truth?

OLIVER. Well, I wouldn't want you to dress it up. What have I got!

DOCTOR. Six months.

OLIVER. It takes six months to cure a social disease?

DOCTOR. What you have is not social, Mister Doe. It's incurable.

OLIVER. What is it!

DOCTOR. Leukemia.

OLIVER. From a toilet seat?

DOCTOR. More likely from your ancestors. It's one of those things they brought over on the Mayflower.

OLIVER. Leukemia!

DOCTOR. If you had only come to me fifteen years ago.

OLIVER. I couldn't. I was only six.

DOCTOR. I might have been able to do something. Now? Well, shall I be honest?

OLIVER. No. Just give me a hint.

DOCTOR. I'm afraid it's terminal.

OLIVER. What does that mean?

DOCTOR. It's the end of the line. It's where the train stops.

OLIVER. You mean . . . you mean I've got to get off?

DOCTOR. I wish I could give you a return ticket.

OLIVER. Can't you keep me on the train?

DOCTOR. Not for longer than six months.

OLIVER. Not even 'till Christmas?

DOCTOR. I'm afraid not.

OLIVER. Labor Day?

DOCTOR. I'm a physician. Not a magician.

OLIVER. You mean there's nothing science can do?

DOCTOR. Oh, no! Science has made wonderful strides. We are now able to predict almost to the minute what your life expectancy will be.

OLIVER. That's wonderful. But what about a cure?

DOCTOR. In a few years—who knows?

OLIVER. In a few years—who cares?

DOCTOR. You've plenty of time to put your house in order.
OLIVER. I live in a furnished room. Ten minutes is ample.
DOCTOR. Look at it this way, son. You made it this far. And you've six more glorious months to live.
OLIVER. You couldn't make it eight? My mother will be on Social Security then.
DOCTOR. I can't turn the clock back.
OLIVER. I just want you to wind it a little.
DOCTOR. Naurally, you'll want to notify your nearest of kin.
OLIVER. No! No! Not anybody. I don't want people sorry for me.
DOCTOR. It's your life.
OLIVER. What's left of it.
DOCTOR. Come back next week. We'll talk.
OLIVER. No thank you. (*He stumbles to the door. The Doctor picks up his report again. Oliver staggers to the outer door, eyes glazed. Anita stops him.*)
ANITA. Oh, Mister Doe.
OLIVER. (*Stops and turns.*) Yes?
ANITA. Would you like to pay your bill now?
OLIVER. What?
ANITA. That's two office visits at fifteen dollars a visit and twenty five dollars for laboratory tests and five dollars delivery charge. That's sixty dollars, if you don't mind.
OLIVER. (*Suddenly shouts.*) WELL, I DO MIND! I sit here for over thirty minutes and the doctor actually sees me for thirty seconds. At that rate, I only owe him fifty cents and that's all I'm damn-well going to play. (*Slams some coins down, McSwain looks from Oliver's paper.*)
BILL. (*Rises.*) Now, look here, fella—don't talk to the little lady like that. Pay your bill.
OLIVER. (*Shoves him roughly back down on the bench.*) You looking for trouble, Mister?
BILL. (Cowed.) No. I was only . . .
OLIVER. Then mind your own business. I'll take care of this dumb bitch myself.
ANITA. (*Rises.*) Would you like me to call the police?
OLIVER. Would you like me to kick your butt over your left shoulder?

35

ANITA. (*Sits quickly.*) Well, if you feel that way, I'll send a bill, Mister Doe.

OLIVER. You do that. And I'll send you a bill for the time I've waited here.

ANITA. Whatever you say, sir.

OLIVER. (*Turns to McSwain.*) What do you think you're doing?

BILL. Just reading the paper.

OLIVER. Well, that happens to be my paper.

BILL. (*Hands it back quickly.*) Sorry—I didn't know.

OLIVER. Next time—ask.

BILL. I will. My mistake.

OLIVER. (*To Anita.*) You got anything else to say?

ANITA. No, sir.

OLIVER. Then shut up! (*He picks up his alarm clock and stalks out of the office.*)

BILL. What do you suppose is bugging him?

ANITA. Paranoid. Don't pay to argue with them.

BILL. I know. I've run into that type before. They're killers.

ANITA. Pays to play safe.

BILL. You can say that again. They don't seem to care if they live or die. Like rattle snakes.

ANITA. I never argue with them. You can't tell what they'll do.

BILL. Play it cool and you'll live longer. (*In his office, the doctor leaps to his feet with the report in his hand.*) Anita! (*He races to the door.*)

ANITA. What is it, doctor?

DOCTOR. Stop that man that just left! (*Anita runs to the door.*) Bring him back! There's been a mistake.

ANITA. (*At door.*) He's gone, doctor. Is anything wrong?

BILL. What is it, doc?

DOCTOR. (*To Anita.*) You gave me the wrong report!

ANITA. It said "John Doe."

DOCTOR. (*Indicates report.*) But he isn't ninety years old.

ANITA. Is it important?

DOCTOR. Yes! I told that boy he was going to die.

BILL. He's ninety now.

DOCTOR. Get his address! Get in touch with him. (*Anita grabs phone book.*)

BILL. He sure acted sore.

DOCTOR. He had a right to be. I gave him six months to live.

36

BILL. That's worse than eating beetles.
DOCTOR. Actually, there's not a thing wrong with that boy.
BILL. I wouldn't like to cross him.
DOCTOR. Hurry, Anita— what's his address!
ANITA. (*Looks up from phone book.*) He hasn't got any.
DOCTOR. He gave you an address, didn't he?
ANITA. The address he gave is the municipal garbage dump.
DOCTOR. Mac—you're F.B.I. Can you find him for us?
BILL. Not at the city dump.
ANITA. What happens if we can't find him?
DOCTOR. He may kill himself. (*They stare at each other.*) Or worse yet . . . somebody else. (*As they exchange looks, the curtain falls.*)

CURTAIN

ACT I

SCENE 4

TIME: *Two hours later.*
PLACE: *The Bank.*
AT RISE: *Before the lights come up, we hear a voice counting in the darkness:*
"Twenty one thousand, three hundred and forty five, twenty one thousand, three hundred and forty six, twenty one thousand, three hundred and forty seven, twenty one thousand . . . etc."
When the scene in the bank fades in, we see Herbie at his desk (instead of Oliver) counting Sophie's pennies as she sits watching diligently.
Millie stands behind her teller window, glancing occasionally at her wrist watch.

HERBIE. —three hundred and forty eight. Twenty one thousand three hundred and forty nine.
SOPHIE. Do you think you'll be able to finish by closing time?
HERBIE. I certainly hope so. (*Turns to Millie.*) Millie, have you any idea why Oliver should take three hours for lunch?

MILLIE. He chews his food very slowly, Mister Henderson.

HERBIE. Well, I'll chew him out when he shows up and it won't be slowly. Twenty one thousand, three hundred and fifty.

MILLIE. He had to see his doctor, Mister Henderson.

HERBIE. What about?

MILLIE. It's something I don't think I should talk about outside of the safety vault.

HERBIE. He'll need a doctor when I'm thru with him. Where was I?

SOPHIE. Twenty one thousand, three hundred and fifty.

HERBIE. (*Resumes counting.*) Twenty one thousand, three hundred and fifty one. He's fired. Twenty one thousand, three hundred and fifty two. On the spot. Twenty one thousand, three hundred and fifty three. No—I'll wait 'till he's finished counting. Twenty one thousand, three hundred and fifty four. (*Oliver enters. Again, he is hardly recognizable. This time he is model of sartorial perfection. Aside from his dashing new suit, he wears a rakish homburg and sports a cane. They stare, slack-jawed, as he swaggers over to Herbie's desk.*)

MILLIE. Oliver—is that you?

SOPHIE. Oliver—is that you?

HERBIE. Oliver—is that you?

OLIVER. There's an echo in here.

MILLIE. Oliver—it can't be you.

OLIVER. Who the hell does it look like?

MILLIE. Johnny Carson.

OLIVER. That's right. I told the clerk I wanted to look like Johnny Carson. Snug but not smug.

HERBIE. (*Awed.*) Where did you get those clothes?

OLIVER. If you've got the right credit cards, you can charge anything. Even your own funeral. Didn't you know that, fat-head?

HERBIE. What did you call me?

SOPHIE. Fat-head.

HERBIE. You're drunk.

OLIVER. You're right.

HERBIE. You're fired.

OLIVER. You're wrong. I quit.

HERBIE. You quit!

OLIVER. You're right.

MILLIE. Oliver—what happened?

38

OLIVER. Who cares?

SOPHIE. Who's going to count my pennies?

OLIVER. Why don't you count them yourself, you dehydrated old pitless prune?

SOPHIE. What did you call me!

HERBIE. A dehydrated old pitless prune.

SOPHIE. I heard him. Fire him!

HERBIE. I just did.

MILLIE. Oliver—you're throwing your life away!

OLIVER. That's right. And it's wonderful.

HERBIE. Oliver Pankey—get your towel and your false cuffs and get out of this bank.

OLIVER. (*Puts up his fists.*) Make me, blubber butt.

SOPHIE. Are you going to let him talk to you that way?

HERBIE. I certainly am not. (*To Millie.*) Millie, go to the corner and call the cop.

MILLIE. He won't come—he's a traffic cop.

OLIVER. So you'll just have to try to throw me out. (*Takes off his coat and hands it to Sophie.*) Hold this. (*To Herbie.*) Are you ready?

HERBIE. Just what do you think you're going to do?

OLIVER. Beat hell out of you.

HERBIE. (*Keeping the desk between them.*) Oliver—this is a bank—you don't settle accounts this way. Remember where you are.

SOPHIE. (*To Herbie.*) And you remember where you are—twenty one thousand, three hundred and fifty four.

HERBIE. Millie—say something to him.

MILLIE. Did you have a good lunch, Oliver?

HERBIE. Tell him I can't fight him. I'm a vice president.

MILLIE. Oliver, don't hit him. He's your superior.

OLIVER. He's going to have to prove it. (*They circle the desk.*)

MILLIE. Don't hit him, Oliver—he's forty.

HERBIE. Thirty nine. But I'm not in shape. And I've got temporary bridge work.

OLIVER. I'll make it permanent.

SOPHIE. I'm withdrawing from this bank. Give me my money back.

OLIVER. How would you like it, madam—on your head? (*He takes a bag of her pennies and pours it over her head.*)

SOPHIE. Protect me! Protect my money. I'm a woman. I'm a depositor.

OLIVER. (*Continues to pour coins over her.*) Pennies from heaven.

MILLIE. Oliver—this is bad for the bank.

SOPHIE. Stop him! He's insane. Do something!

OLIVER. (*To Herbie.*) Yes. Stand still and do something, you coward. (*Herbie gets behind Sophie.*)

SOPHIE. Let go of me! You're standing on my pennies.

HERBIE. (*Puts the desk safely between them again.*) Now, old pal, I've always been your friend. I've always given you my key to the men's room any time you've asked, haven't I, Oliver buddy?

OLIVER. Five years of begging just to go to the John.

SOPHIE. Stop walking on my pennies!

OLIVER. And on top of that, you stole my girl!

HERBIE. You can have her back.

OLIVER. I'ts too late.

HERBIE. With a raise. Ten per cent.

OLIVER. Too little.

HERBIE. And a vacation.

OLIVER. I don't want it.

MILLIE. Doesn't anybody want *me*?

HERBIE. Then what do you want, Oliver?

OLIVER. I want to punch you in the nose. (*A fast and furious game of tag ensues between Oliver and Herbie. The police officer enters and stands watching a moment.*)

OFFICER. Can anyone play?

HERBIE. Officer—you're just in time. Arrest that man. He was going to strike me.

OFFICER. (*To Oliver.*) Is that true?

OLIVER. No. I was going to kill him.

OFFICER. What's going on here?

OLIVER. None of your business.

OFFICER. What did you say?

OLIVER. Go find yourself a dope addict.

OFFICER. What's the matter with him?

SOPHIE. He's lost his mind, that's what. And some of my pennies.

HERBIE. He was about to attack me with a deadly weapon—his fists. Arrest him.

OFFICER. What's the trouble, son?

OLIVER. I'm just tired of being pushed around—by him—you—and everybody.

HERBIE. Handcuff him so I can get at him.

SOPHIE. Put him in jail where he belongs.

OFFICER. Look, folks—we got a new policy in the police department . . . reason. (*To Oliver.*) Now, see here, fellow citizen, why don't you be a nice guy. Put on your coat and go make trouble in some other precinct?

OLIVER. I want to see a little police brutality.

OFFICER. Look—don't push me, fella.

OLIVER. I think you're a faggot cop.

OFFICER. You're not going to get me mad. Sticks and stones can break your bones but words can never hurt you.

OLIVER. Go ahead—try to arrest me.

OFFICER. What the hell's come over everybody—begging to be arrested.

OLIVER. Take your gun and shoot me, you big bully.

OFFICER. You trying to get me demoted?

HERBIE. Arrest him.

SOPHIE. Arrest him.

OLIVER. Arrest me.

OFFICER. I dunno—seems to me like everybody now is either mean, mad or unemployed.

SOPHIE. Arrest him!

OFFICER. I should have been a priest.

HERBIE. ARREST HIM!

OFFICER. Or a postman.

HERBIE. Are you going to arrest him?

OFFICER. No! I already filled my quota for this month. (*To Oliver.*) Now, look, boy . . .

OLIVER. Don't call me "boy." Call me Mister Pankey.

OFFICER. All right. Mister Pankey. Why don't you be a nice guy and leave? I'd appreciate it.

OLIVER. Say please.

OFFICER. How about a pint of my blood?

OLIVER. That's not necessary. I'll leave. Cowards make me sick. (*To Herbie.*) But remember this, Mister Blubber Butt, if we ever meet on a street corner and the traffic sign says "Don't walk" . . . don't walk. Run! (*He stalks to the door.*)

41

MILLIE. Oliver?

OLIVER. Yes?

MILLIE. Are you all right?

OLIVER. I haven't got syphilis, if that's what you mean.

SOPHIE. Such talk! In a bank.

MILLIE. What will you do without a job, Oliver?

OLIVER. I'm not going to work again as long as I live.

MILLIE. Where will you go?

OLIVER. To hell!

MILLIE. Could I go with you, Oliver?

OLIVER. Sorry. I've only got a one way ticket. (*Then nobly.*) Well, folks. You've seen the last of Oliver Wendell Pankey.

(*He turns, head held high, and strides out of sight. In a fraction of a second, he returns with his hands over his head, and a revolver in his back. He is followed by the thief with a mask over his eyes.*)

THIEF. This is a stick-up, folks. Everybody reach for the ceiling. (*All hands go up.*) And no funny business.

OFFICER. This would never happen to a postman.

THIEF. Line up by the desk. (*They line up above the desk.*) Don't run for the door. It's locked. (*To Millie.*) Join your buddies We're closed for the day.

MILLIE. (*Hurries from behind the counter.*) Yes, sir. Anything you want, sir. I'm here to serve, sir.

HERBIE. Shut up!

THIEF. Now, let's get down to business. (*Points to sacks of Sophie's pennies.*) What's in them bags?

SOPHIE. Kitty-litter.

OLIVER. Money.

SOPHIE. Shut up.

THIEF. Well, ain't that handy. In a Safeway shopping cart.

SOPHIE. Don't take my money. Take theirs.

THIEF. Shut up! (*To officer.*) You—gimme your gun. Butt first.

OFFICER. Can I have it back when you're done. I've already lost three. (*Hands it over.*) Would you like to know your constitutional rights?

THIEF. I'd like to know where the money is.

OLIVER. In the safety vault.

THIEF. You know the combination?

OLIVER. (*Points to Herbie.*) He does. He has keys to everything.

42

HERBIE. Oliver—where's your loyalty?

OLIVER. I was fired.

THIEF. (Looks around.) You got a hidden camera in here?

HERBIE. Oh, no. We're a small family branch.

OLIVER. He's lying. (Points.) It's right up there.

THIEF. No fooling. (Vanity showing.) Am I on camera?

OLIVER. Center stage.

THIEF. Is it working now?

HERBIE. No.

OLIVER. Yes. I just saw Herbie press the button with his foot.

HERBIE. Accidently!

THIEF. Will I be on T.V.?

HERBIE. No.

OLIVER. Sure.

THIEF. What station? I want my mother to watch.

OLIVER. All of them.

THIEF. High time. I hit fifteen gas stations and not a word. My mother thinks I'm a liar.

OLIVER. She'll see you this time.

THIEF. Good. Let's put on a good show. (Motions with his gun.) Get over here—all of you. (Poses before ceiling camera.) Could you look a little more cowed, please? Look scared! Beg a little. (Flourishes gun.) That's good.

OFFICER. This ain't gonna look good to the commissioner.

THIEF. Let's give it a little more guts. Get on your knees, folks. Plead for your lives. Or your money. I don't care which. Only feel it. (They all fall to their knees except Oliver.) You—get on your knees.

OLIVER. No.

THIEF. Why not?

OLIVER. I've got on a new suit.

THIEF. Get on your knees!

OLIVER. No.

MILLIE. Oliver!

OLIVER. I've been on my knees for the last time in my life.

THIEF. You said it, brother. You want to get killed?

OLIVER. I couldn't care less.

THIEF. Look—cut it out, fella. This looks lousy for my mother. We're on camera.

MILLIE. Oliver, he'll shoot you.

OLIVER. So what? (*To thief.*) Well, why don't you shoot me? It'll make a good scene.

THIEF. *Why* is it, there's always has to be one spoil-sport! Now —get on your knees!

OLIVER. No.

THIEF. You gotta be different.

OLIVER. Shoot me.

THIEF. You some kind of radical?

MILLIE. Oliver, come on down. You'll be with friends.

OLIVER. No.

HERBIE. Oliver—do what he says. He might shoot one of us.

OLIVER. (*To Herbie.*) I hope you know your picture is being taken down there on your knees.

THIEF. I'll give you three. (*Starts to count.*) One . . . two . . . two and a half . . .

OLIVER. Three. Shoot!

THIEF. You want to get me hung, don't you.

OLIVER. (*Walks over and presses against the gun.*) Go ahead. Pull the trigger. I'll give you three.

THIEF. Don't do me no favors.

OLIVER. One . . . two . . . three.

THIEF. You must wanna die. You're nuts.

OLIVER. Pull the trigger!

THIEF. Look, I never shot nothing in my whole life. Not even a rabbit.

OLIVER. You've got to start some time. Go ahead. Bang. Bang.

THIEF. You keep away from me.

OLIVER. (*Pushes against the gun harder.*) Stop stalling. Shoot.

THIEF. (*Backs up.*) You leave me alone.

MILLIE. Oliver—don't. I can't stand it!

OLIVER. Give me that gun. (*Takes gun from him.*) You're never going to use it.

THIEF. Don't shoot me, please! I got a mother in prison. (*The officer quickly recovers his own gun and covers the thief.*)

OFFICER. That's about the bravest act I ever seen. (*To thief.*) Put your hands up.

OLIVER. Wait a minute. I'm not thru with him. (*To thief.*) Get on your knees.

THIEF. Please don't kill me. I'm not worth it.

OLIVER. I'm not going to shoot you. Not if you do what I say. Get on your knees.

THIEF. Sure, fella. Anything you want. (*Gets on his knees.*)

OLIVER. I want a good picture. (*Poses before camera.*) Pray!

THIEF. Pray?

OLIVER. (*Points gun at him.*) Say your prayers!

THIEF. "Now I lay me down to sleep—I pray the Lord—"

OLIVER. That's good enough. Now get up and cringe.

OFFICER. What a shot. This will be all over the front pages.

OLIVER. (*To officer.*) All right. I'm thru with him. You can tell him his constitutional rights, now. (*Surrenders his gun.*)

MILLIE. Oh, Oliver, you saved our lives. All of us.

HERBIE. I was just about to tackle him myself, Oliver.

SOPHIE. I never seen anything like it. Fearless.

OFFICER. (*To thief.*) Take off that mask. (*Points to hidden camera.*) Let's get a mug shot while we're at it. (*He takes a heroic pose and pulls the thief's mask off.*)

OLIVER. IT'S YOU! He's the thief that robbed me this morning. Give me that gun back! (*He trys frantically to get at the thief. The others hold him off.*) I'll kill him. Let me go!

THIEF. (*Hides behind officer.*) Keep him off of me! You're a cop. It's your job to protect me. I got rights.

OLIVER. He took my mother's allowance. And my pants. Let go of me. Let me kill him.

MILLIE. Oliver! You tiger! Stop it. He's caught now!

OFFICER. You'll get your pants back.

SOPHIE. And probably a reward.

HERBIE. And when the bank president sees that film, he'll probably give you your own key to the men's room.

OLIVER. And when he sees you on your knees, he'll probably fire you. (*Puts his coat back on.*)

MILLIE. Oh, Oliver! We'd all be lying here in a pool of blood if it wasn't for you.

SOPHIE. I'll never forget what you done, Oliver.

HERBIE. I couldn't have done it better myself.

OLIVER. Oh, drop dead—all of you.

MILLIE. Oliver—are you mad at us?

OLIVER. I'm mad at the whole damn world. And nobody better get in my way. (*Starts out.*)

MILLIE. Where are you going, Oliver?

OLIVER. To hell.

MILLIE. What'll you do there, Oliver?

OLIVER. Live a little.

MILLIE. What are you going to live on?

OLIVER. Borrowed time.

MILLIE. But you'll have to do *something*.

OLIVER. I will. I may cross the Atlantic in a canoe. Or hi-jack a space missile. Or take up wrestling alligators. I'll find something to pass the time.

MILLIE. But things like that—wouldn't you be afraid?

OLIVER. I'll never be afraid of anything or anybody again. Not for as long as I live. (*He goes out.*)

OFFICER. Man! There goes a wildcat.

HERBIE. A superman.

MILLIE. A saint.

SOPHIE. (*Leering.*) And sexy, too. (*As they stare after Oliver, the curtain falls.*)

CURTAIN

ACT II

Scene 1

TIME: *A few days later.*
PLACE: *The Bank.*
AT RISE: *Oliver, smartly dressed and exuding confidence, sits behind what was formerly Henderson's desk as the man of authority.*
And Herbie, reduced in rank, stands behind Oliver's place at the counter as a "teller."
Millie is seen at her usual station, cashing a check for Anita.

MILLIE. Fives and tens do?
ANITA. Doctor hates old bills. He thinks used money should be worth less. Everything else used is.
MILLIE. Except human beings. The more they're used, the more they're worth. There you are.
ANITA. Thank you. (*Instead of leaving, she crosses to Oliver's desk.*) Excuse me, but are you Mister Pankey, the new bank manager?
OLIVER. (*Points to desk sign.*) That's what it says.
ANITA. I saw your picture in the paper last week.
OLIVER. (*Holds up a protesting hand.*) Sorry—but no autographs during banking hours.
ANITA. (*Stares at him.*) Haven't I seen you somewhere before?
OLIVER. You just said so—in the papers.
ANITA. That's right. And on T.V. too. Well, I just wanted to say I think you were very brave, catching a bank bandit all by yourself.
OLIVER. I just happened to lose my temper.
ANITA. You could have lost your life.
OLIVER. Would that have made any difference?
ANITA. Imagine, not thinking of yourself like that.
OLIVER. You can't live forever.
ANITA. I'll bet you're not scared of anything.

47

OLIVER. Nothing I can think of.

ANITA. You ever heard of Man-eater-McAvoy?

OLIVER. The prize fighter?

ANITA. He's my boy friend. You know what he's scared to death of? Getting his nose broken. Sometimes I wish he would so he'd stop worrying.

OLIVER. Send him around and I'll break it for him.

ANITA. I'll bet you would, too. Well, it's nice meeting a real live hero for a change. All I meet are hypochondriacs.

OLIVER. At least they got something to live for.

ANITA. Funny I get the feeling I know you. But then, if I'd ever met a man like you, I'd never forget.

OLIVER. Thank you.

ANITA. Take care.

OLIVER. I won't. (*She goes out. Herbie leans over the counter.*)

HERBIE. Excuse me, Mister Pankey, but could I speak to you for a moment?

OLIVER. Is it important?

HERBIE. To me, sir.

OLIVER. Very well. Make it snappy.

HERBIE. (*Scampers over to Oliver.*) Yes, sir.

OLIVER. What's on your mind, Herbie?

HERBIE. It's about the note you left for me, sir.

OLIVER. What about it?

HERBIE. Well, it's a little difficult for me at this time to take a ten per cent cut.

OLIVER. You're loyal to the bank, aren't you?

HERBIE. Oh, yes, sir. Yes, indeed. But since my position here has gone down, my expenses have gone up.

OLIVER. And for the bank, too. You realize that, don't you?

HERBIE. Oh, yes, sir. But since those hidden camera shots were shown on T.V.—my mother has cut off my allowance.

OLIVER. Would you like to leave us?

HERBIE. Oh, no, sir. When you've become president of the bank, well, I hope to move up again.

OLIVER. Then stick around. There'll be a vacancy in about six months.

HERBIE. (*Eagerly.*) You're sure?

OLIVER. I'm positive.

HERBIE. You'll be leaving us?

48

OLIVER. Permanently.

HERBIE. To move higher up?

OLIVER. Much higher.

HERBIE. I must say, I wish I were you.

OLIVER. So do I.

HERBIE. You've made me feel much better.

OLIVER. That's one of us. Now, anything else?

HERBIE. Yes, sir. Could I have the key to the men's room?

OLIVER. (*Hands key to him.*) Ten minutes is the maximum.

HERBIE. Yes, sir. I cut off thirty seconds yesterday.

OLIVER. Well, don't cut yourself.

HERBIE. No, sir. (*He glances at his watch and dashes off.*)

MILLIE. (*Leans over her counter.*) Oliver?

OLIVER. What did you want, Miss Milhaus?

MILLIE. I just wanted to congratulate you.

OLIVER. On this job? I just took it for six months to help the bank.

MILLIE. I don't mean that. I mean what you did at the zoo Sunday.

OLIVER. I just happened to be there. If it hadn't been me, it would have been someone else.

MILLIE. But you're the one that risked your life again. That's twice in one week that your name has been on the front page.

OLIVER. There are always disasters on the front page. It's no honor to be one of them.

MILLIE. If you're not careful, you're going to end up a national hero.

OLIVER. I saw that little brat crawl over the railing. Somebody had to pull him out of the cage. I happened to be closest.

MILLIE. But you were the one that *did* something. You saved him from the jaws of death. You—Oliver Pankey.

OLIVER. Maybe I should have let that gorilla eat him. He'll probably grow up to be a delinquent anyhow.

MILLIE. Weren't you afraid?

OLIVER. Of what?

MILLIE. Well, that gorilla could have reached out and grabbed you, too.

OLIVER. He did. That's when I bit him. I don't know why the newspapers had to make so much of it.

MILLIE. When a man bites a gorilla, that's news, Oliver.

49

OLIVER. Well, at least it made him let go of the little boy.

MILLIE. In my whole life long, Oliver, I've never met anybody who bit a gorilla.

OLIVER. It's no treat. He tasted like a truck driver's sour old glove.

MILLIE. Did you hurt your teeth?

OLIVER. No. But the zoo keeper warned me that gorillas could die from a human bite. We're very poisonous.

MILLIE. Do you know what they called you on the T.V. news this morning? Mister Fearless. Aren't you proud?

OLIVER. Why? Sounds like a detergent.

MILLIE. Well, I just wish I could have seen it. I'd have fainted.

OLIVER. Six people did. One woman and five men.

MILLIE. Just goes to show. (*At this point, Bill McSwain enters and crosses to Oliver's desk.*)

BILL. Mister Pankey?

OLIVER. Yes?

BILL. I'm with the F.B.I. (*Shows him a badge.*)

OLIVER. What can I do for you?

BILL. I'm looking for a certain man.

OLIVER. Who?

BILL. Well, to be perfectly frank—you.

OLIVER. You're looking for me?

BILL. Well, let's say—a man of your caliber.

OLIVER. What does that mean?

BILL. May I talk to you?

OLIVER. Why not?

BILL. My name is McSwain.

OLIVER. You ought to know.

BILL. (*Sits. Then stares at Oliver.*) Haven't I seen you somewhere before?

OLIVER. In the papers.

BILL. No. Somewhere else.

OLIVER. Somebody who looked like me?

BILL. Not really. Anyhow, my department wants to make you a proposition.

OLIVER. Why?

BILL. We've been reading about you in the news.

OLIVER. What's that got to do with the F.B.I.?

BILL. Well, to be perfectly frank, we've come to the bank here to ask your help.

OLIVER. The F.B.I. needs money?

BILL. We need a man with your guts.

OLIVER. What would you do with my guts?

BILL. Two months ago, a Federal armored truck was robbed of six million dollars of government money. Maybe you read about it.

OLIVER. Of course I read about it. Two guards were killed.

BILL. Exactly. And the hi-jackers got away. There was one witness and he disappeared.

OLIVER. Killed?

BILL. No. Hiding. From what we can learn, he's afraid of being killed. That's why he hasn't come forward to make an identification.

OLIVER. What's that got to do with me?

BILL. We want to use you.

OLIVER. For what?

BILL. A sitting duck.

OLIVER. What does that mean?

BILL. We want to announce that you were that witness and that you've come forward to identify the criminals.

OLIVER. Why me?

BILL. Because you're the only man we've come across with the courage and guts to be a sitting duck for us.

OLIVER. But how could I identify those killers when I've never seen them?

BILL. You won't have to. And they don't know that. But the moment we publicize that you were the only witness, they'll come out of hiding to gun you down.

OLIVER. Oh.

BILL. That's right.

OLIVER. You want to use me for bait?

BILL. Correct.

OLIVER. Like a piece of swiss cheese?

BILL. You get it.

OLIVER. Full of holes.

BILL. You'll be protected night and day by undercover agents. Some of them will be posing as panhandlers, dope addicts, prostitutes, peddlers, hippies, women, even cops. You won't know them.

OLIVER. Then I won't know who the killers are either, will I?

BILL. But we will. And the moment they start shooting at you, we nab 'em.

OLIVER. And if they get me first?

BILL. We'll see that your reward goes to whoever you name.

OLIVER. Reward? You mean I get a medal? Posthumously?

BILL. Naturally, you'll get part of the reward money once the loot is recovered.

OLIVER. Oh.

BILL. You could be a rich man.

OLIVER. Or a dead duck.

BILL. Can we count on you?

OLIVER. What can I lose?

BILL. (*Pumps his hand.*) I knew we could. You're the only man we could find completely without fear. Tell me—is it true you bit a gorilla at the zoo?

OLIVER. I guess that was cowardly of me.

BILL. Cowardly! A six hundred pound gorilla!

OLIVER. Well, after all, I'm over twenty one and that gorilla was only six years old.

BILL. They don't make them like you anymore. (*Rises.*) Well, I'll release the news right away. We ought to get some action by tomorrow. Be seeing you, Tarzan. (*He goes out. Millie races to Oliver from behind the counter.*)

MILLIE. Oliver—I heard. Don't do it. Please don't throw your life away because of me!

OLIVER. What are you talking about?

MILLIE. Oh, you don't fool me, Oliver. A woman always knows. But death is no way to cure a broken heart, Oliver.

OLIVER. You're wrinkling my shirt!

MILLIE. Do you think I want your blood on my hands?

OLIVER. Stop pulling—it's silk.

MILLIE. Oh, don't sacrifice your young life for my happiness.

OLIVER. I can use the reward. My mother needs new teeth.

MILLIE. I'm not worth it, Oliver.

OLIVER. You decide.

MILLIE. I broke our engagement and broke your poor heart, didn't I?

OLIVER. It was something else.

MILLIE. I know the truth now, Oliver. Forgive me.

OLIVER. All right.

MILLIE. No. You don't mean it.

OLIVER. I swear!

MILLIE. You really forgive me?

OLIVER. Honest.

MILLIE. Why didn't you speak up this morning and tell me how much I meant to you.

OLIVER. I wasn't dressed.

MILLIE. And now you don't care what happens to you, do you?

OLIVER. No. Yes. No. You don't understand.

MILLIE. Why have you put me on a pedestal, Oliver?

OLIVER. I haven't.

MILLIE. I'm not perfect, you know.

OLIVER. I know.

MILLIE. I didn't mean to inspire you to throw your life away.

OLIVER. Believe me, you never inspired me.

MILLIE. How I must have hurt you. Do you want to cry, Oliver?

OLIVER. In the bank?

MILLIE. And now you want to die, don't you?

OLIVER. What makes you think that?

MILLIE. You bit a gorilla.

OLIVER. Don't remind me. If the gorilla dies, the zoo will sue.

MILLIE. Oliver—if you're shot tomorrow—have you thought what that will do to me? It will kill me.

OLIVER. No one's shooting at you. Yet.

MILLIE. Oliver. I'm going to give you a reason to want to live. (*Takes his hand.*) Come with me to the safety vault.

OLIVER. I can't. Herbie's in the men's room.

MILLIE. Are you going to be in your room tonight, Oliver?

OLIVER. What's he doing all this time?

MILLIE. I will show you that life is worth living.

OLIVER. It's been over ten minutes.

MILLIE. After all, I didn't give you a birthday present.

OLIVER. Nothing takes that long. (*Herbie enters, dejectedly.*) Well, high time.

HERBIE. I'll bet you wonder what kept me.

OLIVER. I hope it was bank business.

HERBIE. I got soap in my eye.

OLIVER. Do you always wash your face when you go to the men's room?

HERBIE. Doesn't everybody?

OLIVER. Never mind. I have a date to play golf with the president. I'm leaving you in charge. (*Starts for door.*)

MILLIE. Oliver—be careful. Don't get hit by a golf ball.

OLIVER. One never knows how one is going—feet or head first. (*He goes out quickly.*)

HERBIE. Some people just have a charmed life. He gets promoted, I get soap in my eye.

MILLIE. Herbie—I've discovered Oliver's secret.

HERBIE. It's no secret. He's got my job.

MILLIE. His hidden secret. He doesn't want to live.

HERBIE. How do you know that?

MILLIE. A woman's intuition.

HERBIE. You could be wrong.

MILLIE. Why would he bite a gorilla?

HERBIE. He's not fastidious.

MILLIE. No. He wants to die. Herbie, you've got to help.

HERBIE. You want me to kill him?

MILLIE. No. Save him from himself.

HERBIE. Why me?

MILLIE. Because you and me are to blame.

HERBIE. For what!

MILLIE. For what happened in the safety vault.

HERBIE. I should have been stronger. Especially in the safety vault.

MILLIE. Our engagement has broken his heart. Do you know what's going to happen to him?

HERBIE. He's going to be president.

MILLIE. He's going to be shot.

HERBIE. Can we count on it?

MILLIE. He's offered himself as a sitting duck for the F.B.I. Tomorrow, killers will try to gun him down.

HERBIE. Tomorrow? Good Friday?

MILLIE. He may never see the sun set. All because life is meaningless without me. It makes me so proud.

HERBIE. He told you this?

MILLIE. He didn't have to. Women know these things. That's why we're women.

HERBIE. What are you going to do?
MILLIE. Save him. It's the least I can do. But I wanted to be honest with you. I wanted to hold my head up. Afterwards.
HERBIE. I don't know what the hell you're talking about.
MILLIE. (Shouts.) I'M TALKING ABOUT SAVING OLIVER WENDELL PANKEY'S LIFE!
HERBIE. How?
MILLIE. (Seductive again.) Well may you ask. (She sidles over to the counter, arch and feline, a slow smile of martyrdom on her face.) The only way I know. A woman's way. (As she stares out the door, heavy-lidded and dedicated, Herbie turns to the audience and shrugs dumbly.)

CURTAIN

ACT II

SCENE 2

TIME: Next morning.
PLACE: Oliver's room.
AT RISE: There are now colorful curtains in Oliver's room. There is also a hi-fi set, a telephone and gay pillows on the sofa.
Oliver, in an elaborate silk robe, has music playing at full volume. He proceeds to open a box on the sofa and take out a new suit. He looks at it approvingly and hangs it up.
He then opens a box of fresh flowers and puts them in a vase after throwing the old ones out the window.
There is a pounding on the door. He turns off the set and opens it.

OLIVER. Oh, I thought you were Millie again.
BILL. (Enters swiftly carrying a window dummy—or card-board cutout of a man.) Pull the curtain!
OLIVER. (Pulls curtain.) What have you got there?
BILL. You.
OLIVER. Me?
BILL. It's supposed to look like you. Anything happen last night?

55

OLIVER. Almost.

BILL. What?

OLIVER. Millie kept knocking at my door.

BILL. Did you let her in?

OLIVER. No. I thought I ought to get a good night's sleep if I was going to be shot at this morning.

BILL. Did anybody shoot at you this morning?

OLIVER. I haven't been up long.

BILL. Good. That's why I've brought this. (*Sets dummy up by window.*) Word got out last night. The shooting could start any minute.

OLIVER. I haven't had my orange juice yet.

BILL. This dummy might draw their first attempt to get you.

OLIVER. Whose idea was that?

BILL. Counter-intelligence.

OLIVER. Who are they?

BILL. Just the best brains we have. They planned the Bay of Pigs.

OLIVER. What makes you think those killers will try to get me this early?

BILL. Two men just rented a room in the building right across from yours. Very suspicious. Paid in advance.

OLIVER. What makes you think they're the killers?

BILL. They were carrying violin cases.

OLIVER. Maybe they were musicians.

BILL. Musicians don't get up before noon. You have to know these things.

OLIVER. You think guns were in the violin cases?

BILL. You don't bend over to carry a violin.

OLIVER. Then why didn't you arrest them?

BILL. It's illegal. They have to commit a crime first.

OLIVER. You wait until they start shooting?

BILL. That's right. But don't worry. We've got thirteen trucks surrounding this building—all filled with counter-intelligence agents.

OLIVER. Won't that make the killers suspicious?

BILL. Not a chance. They're disguised as *Good Humor* trucks. (*Peers out the window.*)

OLIVER. What do I do?

BILL. Sit tight. And don't go near the window. (*He jiggles the*

56

dummy and waits. There is a knock at the door. Bill quickly draws a revolver. He signals for silence.)

BILL. I'll hide and keep you covered. (*Opens closet door.*) If it's a *Good Humor* man, he's one of ours. (*Hides in closet. Oliver opens the door. Sophie enters carrying a tray. She has made a futile attempt to look alluring.*)

SOPHIE. I brought you some breakfast.

OLIVER. I hope you didn't go to any trouble.

SOPHIE. Nothing at all. Just a little fresh orange juice, strawberries and cream, half a grapefruit, oatmeal, mushroom omelette, toast, little-pig sausage, blueberry muffins, clover honey, coffee and a vitamin pill.

OLIVER. Oh, you shouldn't have.

SOPHIE. Why not? Since Mister Goggan died, I've missed having a man around to cook for.

OLIVER. It's more than I can eat.

SOPHIE. Don't matter. Handsome young feller like you should have everything he wants. (*Sits and preens.*) You ever been married, Oliver?

OLIVER. Not yet.

SOPHIE. Mister Goggan was fifteen years younger than me. He couldn't have been happier. A feller's smart to marry some one that's settled.

OLIVER. I suppose you're right.

SOPHIE. Glad to see you're sensible. Must get lonely up here by yourself.

OLIVER. I got a new hi-fi set.

SOPHIE. I noticed it. Must have cost a pretty penny.

OLIVER. I didn't ask.

SOPHIE. Lovely tone. I could hear it down in the basement.

OLIVER. Was I playing it too loud?

SOPHIE. Doesn't matter. Anything you want to do is all right with me.

OLIVER. Thank you.

SOPHIE. If you know what I mean.

OLIVER. Some little pig-sausage?

SOPHIE. All you got to do is whistle.

OLIVER. Is this instant oatmeal?

SOPHIE. I can dish it any way you want, Oliver. You want it slow or instant, I can deliver.

OLIVER. (*Rises.*) Well, I got to get dressed now.
SOPHIE. Nothing special you want?
OLIVER. I've got to meet a couple of musicians.
SOPHIE. (*Goes to door.*) I can see you're in a hurry. When
you come home, knock on my door.
OLIVER. Why?
SOPHIE. I'll have something for you.
OLIVER. What?
SOPHIE. I'll let you sample my Apple Pan Dowdy. (*She goes
out. Oliver turns with relief to the closet.*)
OLIVER. Come out. I thought you were supposed to protect me.
BILL. (*Comes out. Points to food.*) Don't eat any more of that!
OLIVER. Why not?
BILL. It may be poisoned. Those killers won't stop at anything.
(*Goes to window with tray.*) We can't take a chance. (*Throws
tray out window. There is a yell from below.*)
VOICE. Hey! Watch it up there!
BILL. (*Peers out window.*) Sorry, Milo.
OLIVER. Aren't you liable to be shot?
BILL. You're right. (*Jerks his head back in.*) That was Milo.
One of ours.
OLIVER. *Good Humor?*
BILL. Top man. Led the landing at Bay of Pigs.
OLIVER. Why didn't you rescue me when that old bag was after
me?
BILL. This is too hush-hush. (*Looks at dummy.*) May be too
dark in here. I'll pull the curtains. (*He draws the curtains aside.*)
Now, we'll see what happens. (*There is a knock at the door. Bill
quickly hides in the closet again.*)
OLIVER. Who is it?
MILLIE. (*Offstage.*) Me. Millie. (*Opens door.*) Well, about
time. I knocked for hours last night.
OLIVER. I sleep with ear plugs.
MILLIE. (*Sees cut-out.*) What's that?
OLIVER. A snapshot. I had it enlarged.
MILLIE. I brought your mail up.
OLIVER. Thanks. I been getting a lot of fan mail. And hate
letters.
MILLIE. Is that your red sports car parked down in front?

OLIVER. (*Opening mail.*) Not exactly. I've just rented it for six months.

MILLIE. Looks fast.

OLIVER. It is. I got it up to a hundred and eighty in the park yesterday. (*Opens next letter.*)

MILLIE. Weren't you afraid of being arrested?

OLIVER. I was. (*Opens wallet to show tickets.*) I've collected fifteen speeding tickets so far. (*He tears them up.*)

MILLIE. Oliver! You'll spend the rest of your life in jail!

OLIVER. Not a chance. (*Waves a letter.*) This will give you a laugh.

MILLIE. Something funny?

OLIVER. Very. A letter from my draft board.

MILLIE. You've been drafted?

OLIVER. That's what they think. (*Tears it up.*)

MILLIE. You'll go to prison!

OLIVER. They won't keep me long.

MILLIE. I have a feeling I don't know you, Oliver. In just a week's time you seem to have grown taller.

OLIVER. Maybe you've grown shorter. What did you want?

MILLIE. Could I sit and talk to you a moment?

OLIVER. Well, I haven't much time. (*They sit on sofa.*)

MILLIE. I made a terrible mistake, Oliver. When I broke our engagement, I didn't know what it would do to you. Do you want me back, Oliver?

OLIVER. It wouldn't be fair to you, Millie.

MILLIE. Don't think of Herbie. I'll break my engagement to him.

OLIVER. You'd ruin his life.

MILLIE. But you have no one, Oliver. He has his wife and children.

OLIVER. He needs you.

MILLIE. But I can't stand by and let you destroy yourself over me.

OLIVER. I've nothing to offer you, Millie. Believe me.

MILLIE. Oliver, I've run a terrible risk coming to your room like this while I'm still engaged to Herbie. He's insanely jealous—a wild man. But I had to save you if I could.

OLIVER. No one can save me, Millie. No one. That's all I can say. (*Rises.*) Now if you'll excuse me, I have to brush my teeth. (*He gets down on his hands and knees and crawls under the win-*

dow sill to get to the bathroom. Millie sits for a moment, frustrated. She then pulls a button off her blouse.)

MILLIE. Oh, Oliver?

OLIVER. *(Returns to door with toothbrush in his mouth.)* Yes?

MILLIE. I've busted a button off my blouse.

OLIVER. I'll get you a safety pin.

MILLIE. No—just get me a needle and thread. *(Starts taking her blouse off.)* I'll sew it back on.

OLIVER. *(Crawls back under the window sill to bed table.)* What color thread?

MILLIE. You got red?

OLIVER. What shade? Chinese or turkey?

MILLIE. Turkey red if you've got it.

OLIVER. My mother keeps me supplied.

MILLIE. She teach you to sew?

OLIVER. No, my Father. He was a tailor. *(Hands her needle and thread.)*

MILLIE. I'll bet you've got everything a girl needs, Oliver.

OLIVER. Well, if you need anything special, I've got a thimble.

MILLIE. No, but you can thread the needle for me.

OLIVER. Didn't you ever learn to thread a needle?

MILLIE. I'm near-sighted.

OLIVER. Oh, well—give me the needle.

MILLIE. Now, I don't want you to do everything. I'll hold the needle and you can thread it.

OLIVER. *(Sits beside her.)* It's a dumb way to thread a needle.

MILLIE. I like to feel I'm helping. *(Holds needle on a level with her breasts.)* I think this is the first time I've ever been this close to the top of your head, Oliver.

OLIVER. Hold the needle still.

MILLIE. You certainly smell good.

OLIVER. It's mint toothpaste.

MILLIE. Lots nicer than Herbie.

OLIVER. I've never smelled him.

MILLIE. You don't have dandruff, either.

OLIVER. Don't wiggle.

MILLIE. Wait—I'll brace my hands steady. *(She holds the needle firmly between her breasts.)* This'll make it easier for you.

OLIVER. Could you look the other way?

MILLIE. Why?

OLIVER. You're breathing on my glasses.

MILLIE. Oliver?

OLIVER. Yes.

MILLIE. Could I ask you something very personal?

OLIVER. Why not?

MILLIE. Have you ever been this close to a girl like this before?

OLIVER. In the subway.

MILLIE. I mean—well—have you ever slept with a—well, you know—a woman? *(She bends farther back so that Oliver is forced to lean over her.)*

OLIVER. Hundreds of times.

MILLIE. Who?

OLIVER. My mother.

MILLIE. Your mother!

OLIVER. I was afraid of the dark.

MILLIE. I mean—anyone else?

OLIVER. My father.

MILLIE. Oliver, imagine me beside you instead of your father. Think of what it would be like.

OLIVER. Why should I want to imagine you as my father?

MILLIE. *(Now almost prone.)* Oliver?

OLIVER. Yes?

MILLIE. Are you afraid?

OLIVER. Yes.

MILLIE. What are you afraid of?

OLIVER. I'm afraid you're going to stick yourself with that needle.

MILLIE. *(Straightens up, pushing him back.)* This isn't going to work. Look—you hold the needle. Give me the thread. I'll find the eye.

OLIVER. Isn't this a lot of trouble to go to for a button?

MILLIE. I don't like to start something I can't finish. *(She begins to force Oliver slowly backwards.)* Why are you breathing so hard?

OLIVER. You've got your elbow in my stomach.

MILLIE. *(Moistens end of thread.)* That all?

OLIVER. No, you ought to start with a new piece of thread. I had the end of that in my mouth.

MILLIE. I like it. Mint.

OLIVER. Millie.

MILLIE. Yes?

OLIVER. Looking at you this close—could I tell you something?

MILLIE. What, Oliver?

OLIVER. You look cross-eyed.

MILLIE. You're not giving me much co-operation, Oliver!

OLIVER. I offered you a safety pin.

MILLIE. I thought it would be nice if we could do something together, Oliver.

OLIVER. But I'm not dressed. (*There is a sudden knock at the door. Both straighten up quickly.*) Who is it?

HERBIE. (*Offstage.*) Herbie Henderson.

MILLIE. Herbie! Hide me, Oliver. He's insanely jealous. He'll never believe I just lost a button.

OLIVER. Get in the bathroom—quick! (*She grabs her blouse and flees into the bathroom. Oliver opens the door. Herbie enters.*)

HERBIE. Could I talk to you?

OLIVER. Well, I'm kind of busy.

HERBIE. This won't take long. Are we alone?

OLIVER. Why?

HERBIE. I heard voices.

OLIVER. I had the T.V. on.

HERBIE. I'm not interupting anything, am I?

OLIVER. No. I was just threading a needle.

HERBIE. (*Points to facsimile at window.*) What's that?

OLIVER. I do cut-outs. I got some scissors for Christmas.

HERBIE. Shows talent.

OLIVER. What did you want to see me about, Herbie?

HERBIE. Millie.

OLIVER. What about her?

HERBIE. Well, I'm engaged to her, you know.

OLIVER. Yes, I know. And you know. And Millie knows. But there's one thing I'd like to know.

HERBIE. What?

OLIVER. Does your wife know?

HERBIE. My wife is suffering from an incurable disease.

OLIVER. Leukemia?

HERBIE. Jealousy.

OLIVER. Does she know about Millie?

HERBIE. If she knew, she'd kill me. Or Millie.

OLIVER. Look. I've got an idea. You don't want her to kill Millie, do you?

HERBIE. Of course not.

OLIVER. Then tell her you're in love with me and let her kill me.

HERBIE. You keep talking as if you don't want to live.

OLIVER. Make me an offer.

HERBIE. That's exactly why I'm here. Millie is a wonderful girl. Pretty—young—competent—

OLIVER. But she can't thread a needle.

HERBIE. You'll admit, she's everything a man could want, won't you?

OLIVER. I suppose so.

HERBIE. (*Falls to his knees.*) Then take her off my hands!

OLIVER. You want to dump her?

HERBIE. In the river—on her head—anything to get rid of her.

OLIVER. I don't think that's very nice—with the rivers all polluted.

HERBIE. Get me off the hook. You could work it. You're not afraid of anything.

OLIVER. What could I do?

HERBIE. I don't know. I haven't got an evil mind. Fix it so I could catch you trying to seduce her. Get her blouse off or something so I could break in and break our engagement.

OLIVER. (*Glances toward bathroom.*) You're going to be sorry you said those things.

HERBIE. She's not bright enough to suspect anything.

OLIVER. She might surprise you.

HERBIE. How do I get in these messes!

OLIVER. You talk too much.

HERBIE. What can I do? I want to be set free!

OLIVER. Stand in front of the window there a moment.

HERBIE. What for?

OLIVER. You might get your wish. (*At this point, Millie steps out of the bathroom.*)

MILLIE. So that's all I mean to you, Herbie Henderson.

HERBIE. Why didn't you tell me she was in there!

OLIVER. You didn't ask.

HERBIE. What happened to your blouse?

OLIVER. She busted her button.

MILLIE. And now I know the truth. (*Hands Herbie a bottle.*) And with this I hereby set you free, Herbert.

HERBIE. (*Looks down at the bottle.*) What is it?

63

MILLIE. Empty.

HERBIE. What was in it?

MILLIE. My pride. I swallowed it.

HERBIE. She's taken sleeping pills!

MILLIE. Be happy, Herbert. (*With a sad smile, she sinks dreamily to the floor.*)

HERBIE. She swallowed the whole bottle.

OLIVER. Don't be silly. She couldn't swallow the bottle. It's too big.

HERBIE. She's dying! (*Kneels beside her.*) But she's still breathing.

OLIVER. That's a good sign.

HERBIE. We've got to save her. What shall we do, Oliver!

OLIVER. Mix a lot of soapy water.

HERBIE. She needs a doctor—not a bath.

OLIVER. The thing to do is make her throw up.

HERBIE. In here?

OLIVER. Why not?

HERBIE. Well, it's a small room.

OLIVER. She's not going to die.

HERBIE. After what she's swallowed!

OLIVER. I never heard of anybody dying from vitamin pills.

HERBIE. Vitamin pills?

OLIVER. I keep them in that bottle so no one will steal them.

HERBIE. Then she's not going to die?

OLIVER. She's taken enough vitamin pills to keep her alive for fifty years.

HERBIE. (*Promptly drops her.*) But she's passed out. Won't she be sick?

OLIVER. Just embarrassed.

HERBIE. Well, are you going to do something?

OLIVER. (*Sits on sofa.*) Yes. I'm going to thread this goddamn needle.

HERBIE. Do you realize what my wife will do if this gets back to her?

OLIVER. Divorce you?

HERBIE. Permanently. She's just crazy enough to get a gun and try to shoot me. (*At this point, there is a burst of gun-fire at the window. The dummy's head is shot off and tumbles to the floor. Millie's eyes pop open.*)

MILLIE. My God!

HERBIE. My wife!

BILL. (*Bolts from the closet.*) My *Good Humor* men! (*Dashes out the door.*)

OLIVER. Must have been those musicians.

HERBIE. What the hell is going on around here!

MILLIE. (*Sitting up.*) Yes. What the hell is going on around here!

OLIVER. Didn't you see? I just had my head shot off. (*As he calmly proceeds to thread his needle, the curtain falls.*)

CURTAIN

ACT II

Scene 3

TIME: *Monday.*

PLACE: *The bank.*

AT RISE: *Herbie is seen beside Oliver's desk, sorting out the morning mail.*

After a moment, Millie enters. She passes Herbie without speaking.

HERBIE. Good morning, Millie.

MILLIE. I am not speaking to you, Mister Henderson. (*She goes to her teller's window.*)

HERBIE. I'll bet you think I'm a dirty skunk.

MILLIE. I said that I was not speaking to you.

HERBIE. I told my wife about you, Millie.

MILLIE. YOU WHAT!

HERBIE. She wants to meet you.

MILLIE. She wants to meet me!

HERBIE. She said she wants to meet anyone who'd commit suicide over me.

MILLIE. I thought you said she was in an institution!

HERBIE. She is. Godiva Health Institute. She's overweight.

MILLIE. You had no right to talk about me behind my back.

HERBIE. I had to tell someone. I was so proud that you'd swallowed a whole bottle full of vitamin pills because of me.

65

MILLIE. I have a deficiency, that's all.

HERBIE. You must love me very much, Millie.

MILLIE. I hate you.

HERBIE. She'll give me a divorce, Millie.

MILLIE. Your wife agreed?

HERBIE. No—my mother. She controls the money.

MILLIE. What did your wife say?

HERBIE. She agreed, too—if we'll take the children.

MILLIE. Did it ever occur to you that I might not want you, Mister Henderson?

HERBIE. No. Why should it? (*They both look up as the police officer enters. He goes to Oliver's desk and peers under it. He then glances cautiously around the bank. He goes back to the front door and calls out.*)

OFFICER. All clear, Mac. Security checked. (*He stands aside as Bill, like a palace guard, escorts Oliver to his desk.*)

BILL. (*Salutes.*) Safely delivered!

OLIVER. Some security. You let the killers slip right thru your fingers.

BILL. So we made a tactical error. But we're not discouraged. At least we know now that they're out to get you.

OLIVER. I don't see how you could let them get away. You had the whole block surrounded.

BILL. How did we know they'd pose as *Good Humor* men, too?

OLIVER. You're going to give ice-cream a bad name.

BILL. But we're ready next time they show their hand.

OLIVER. You think they'll try again?

BILL. Any minute.

OLIVER. Here?

BILL. They're desperate now. But we're prepared. I've got this whole area saturated with undercover agents.

OLIVER. What are they posing as this time?

BILL. Garbage collectors. We never use the same disguise twice.

OLIVER. Won't so many garbage men look suspicious?

BILL. Why?

OLIVER. Well, there's a garbage strike.

BILL. Killers aren't that smart.

OLIVER. Suppose they pose as garbage men, too?

BILL. They can't.

OLIVER. Why not?

BILL. They'd have to have union cards.

OLIVER. Oh, well that's different.

BILL. But the chief wants you to have a gun. (*Takes out a revolver.*)

OLIVER. (*Stares at it.*) Is it filled?

BILL. Oh, it's loaded all right.

OLIVER. That's good. It's always an empty gun that kills someone.

BILL. Did you ever have one of these?

OLIVER. Sure. When I was a kid.

BILL. You had a pistol?

OLIVER. Made of glass with candy in it.

BILL. Well, this is loaded with lead and it's very indigestible.

OLIVER. What if I have to use it?

BILL. You know how, don't you?

OLIVER. Sure. You aim it at what you want to hit, then close your eyes and pull the trigger.

BILL. I better show you. Stick it in your belt.

OLIVER. (*Puts it in his belt, center, barrel down and butt sticking out.*) I hope it doesn't go off.

BILL. No—no. Under your coat to the side. That comfortable?

OLIVER. I think I tore my underwear.

BILL. Now. I'll be the killer. I come at you. When I say "Hands up"—I want you to draw.

OLIVER. A check, a painting or the pistol?

BILL. Draw a bead on me. O.K. hands up! (*Oliver struggles valiantly to get the pistol out of his belt while Bill waits.*) You know something? You've been dead ten minutes.

OLIVER. My belt's too tight.

BILL. Yank it out! (*Oliver gets the pistol out, wincing.*) What's the matter?

OLIVER. I scratched my stomach.

BILL. Now—when you fire, do it like a professional. Squat. (*He demonstrates, assuming the position of a Sumo wrestler.*)

OLIVER. That's funny.

BILL. Why?

OLIVER. You look like a cowboy without a horse under him.

BILL. You stand like this to reduce the target area if he shoots first.

OLIVER. Is he going to shoot between my legs?

BILL. That's to give you balance, too. Now, aim for a vital area.

OLIVER. Which end is that?

BILL. Aim for the elbow. The idea is to take him alive. When we kill a bystander, it's embarrassing for the bureau.

OLIVER. I know. And we lose a depositor.

BILL. All right. Now, I'm your killer again. (*As he squats, Sophie enters the bank and stops.*) "Hands up!"

OLIVER. (*Squats and aims the pistol.*) Bang! Bang! You're dead. (*Bill grabs his elbow in mock pain.*) You got me! (*He sinks to the floor.*) Don't kill me, pal. I'll turn state's evidence.

SOPHIE. I wonder if this is the sort of bank where I should keep my money?

BILL. (*Gets up.*) This is just a dry run, madam.

OLIVER. Without blood.

SOPHIE. I don't know what the world is coming to—what with *Good Humor* men all over the place shooting at each other.

BILL. Well, I'll go out and check on my garbage men. (*Goes to door.*) Be careful. Watch out for any strangers that may come into the bank. Protect yourself. Squat! (*He demonstrates again and goes out.*)

SOPHIE. What is he—a frog?

OLIVER. He's my guardian angel. What can I do for you this morning, Miss Goggan?

SOPHIE. Well, what with all this shooting going on, nothing's safe anymore. I got twenty six books of trading stamps I'd like to keep in your deposit vault.

OLIVER. Millie! (*Turns back to Sophie.*) Millie will take care of you. You're being very sensible, Miss Goggan. You could be shot, mugged or run over any minute up here, but in the deposit vault, you can rest assured your trading stamps will be safe.

MILLIE. (*Stops at desk.*) Yes, Mister Pankey?

OLIVER. Show Miss Goggan the way to get to the deposit vault.

MILLIE. This way. (*She goes out with a sexy wiggle. Sophie stares after her.*)

SOPHIE. I haven't been able to walk that way in thirty years. (*She follows Millie out. Oliver sits down and takes bullets out of pistol.*)

OLIVER. Herbie.

HERBIE. Yes, Mister Pankey?

OLIVER. Come here a minute. (*As Herbie comes to the desk, Oliver puts one bullet back in the cylinder.*)

HERBIE. Yes, sir?

OLIVER. Herbie, I've thought of a way we can settle Millie's future.

HERBIE. How?

OLIVER. Russian roulette.

HERBIE. You mean—where there's one bullet and you take turns?

OLIVER. That's right. Fate decides. (*Puts gun to temple.*) Like this. (*Pulls trigger.*) Missed.

HERBIE. (*Backs away.*) You're not suggesting . . .

OLIVER. You and I will play a little game. And whoever loses—wins.

HERBIE. But I don't want to die. I'd rather marry Millie.

OLIVER. What are you afraid of? You can't live forever.

HERBIE. But once you're dead—you're dead forever.

OLIVER. (*Spins cylinder.*) I'll go first.

HERBIE. Don't! Don't!

OLIVER. Why not?

HERBIE. I can't stand noise.

OLIVER. Life is a gamble, Herbie.

HERBIE. Not in a bank.

OLIVER. You get better odds. Six to one. (*Lifts pistol and pulls trigger.*) Blank. See? I get a second chance. Most people don't. Your turn.

HERBIE. (*Flees back to counter.*) I think you're crazy.

OLIVER. To be free of fear is not necessarily crazy, Herbie.

HERBIE. You don't make sense.

OLIVER. What does? (*At this point, a stranger enters. A most oddly dressed stranger. He is bearded, wears a long dark overcoat, dark glasses and a soft felt hat with the rim pulled down. To anyone less suspicious than Oliver, he would appear to be a very dangerous character. He crosses to Oliver carrying a black valise.*)

STRANGER. Are you Mister Pankey?

OLIVER. At your service.

STRANGER. Mister Oliver Pankey?

OLIVER. That's right. May I help you?

STRANGER. I have a little business to do with you.

OLIVER. Splendid. May I ask how you knew my name?

STRANGER. I saw your picture in the paper.

OLIVER. And what can I do for you?

STRANGER. I've a suit-case here I'd like to leave.

OLIVER. Well, the girl is with another customer down in the vault right now, but I'll take care of you. (*Takes out a form.*) Your name, please?

STRANGER. Ripper.

OLIVER. And your first name?

STRANGER. Jack.

OLIVER. What business are you in, Mister Ripper?

STRANGER. I'm an exterminator.

OLIVER. Termites?

STRANGER. Rats.

OLIVER. Business good?

STRANGER. Gets better every minute.

OLIVER. Shall I insure the contents?

STRANGER. I don't think it's worth it.

OLIVER. May I inquire what's in the valise?

STRANGER. An invention of mine.

OLIVER. Oh. Would I be nosey to ask what?

STRANGER. A rat exterminator.

OLIVER. Well, it will be perfectly safe here. Will you sign this please, Mister Ripper. (*He signs.*) The girl will be here in just a moment.

STRANGER. I don't think I'll wait. (*Rises.*)

OLIVER. It will just be a minute.

STRANGER. I got a date on the other side of town. (*He hurries out.*)

OLIVER. But, Mister Ripper. You didn't take your receipt.

HERBIE. He certainly seemed to be in a hurry.

OLIVER. Probably had something pressing on his mind. (*Returns to desk. Sits humming a moment. Looks at his watch. Frowns and shakes it.*) Now what!

HERBIE. Anything wrong, Mister Pankey?

OLIVER. Something's happened to my watch. It's ticking too loud. (*Puts it to his ear.*)

HERBIE. I can hear it over here.

OLIVER. I'm glad it isn't paid for yet. They'll certainly hear about this. (*Bill comes racing in to Oliver's desk, breathless and excited.*)

BILL. Oliver, we're in luck. We've discovered two men parked in a car across the street and we think they're the killers we want.

OLIVER. But you're not sure.

BILL. Well, they're watching the bank and they've got violin cases.

OLIVER. Why don't you arrest them?

BILL. They've got to start shooting first. We don't have a crime yet.

OLIVER. Well, they'll just have to wait for me 'till the bank closes. You didn't see a man in a dark overcoat just leave, did you?

BILL. No. Why?

OLIVER. He left a suitcase and didn't take his receipt.

BILL. He what!

OLIVER. (*Points.*) His suitcase. You'd think he'd worry.

BILL. (*Leaps to his feet, backing away.*) GET EVERYBODY OUT OF THE BANK!

OLIVER. Why? It's not time to close.

BILL. It's a time bomb. Get out!

OLIVER. No, it isn't. It's just a rat trap.

BILL. A rat trap doesn't tick!

OLIVER. Well, I'm certainly glad it isn't my watch. (*Millie appears with Sophie.*)

BILL. (*Shouts.*) Don't come in here!

MILLIE. What's the matter?

OLIVER. Somebody forgot his time bomb.

SOPHIE. This bank is certainly going down hill.

BILL. Stay back! It's going up in the air any minute.

SOPHIE. With my money?

BILL. (*At door.*) Oliver—get away from it. You'll be blown up.

OLIVER. Well, that'll get me to heaven quicker than I thought.

BILL. Run, Oliver! I'll send for the demolition squad.

OLIVER. Oh, don't bother. I'll take it apart.

BILL. Are you crazy!

HERBIE. Yes.

OLIVER. Won't you be surprised if it's only a rat trap?

HERBIE. (*At door.*) Won't you if it isn't.

OLIVER. Well, we'll soon find out. (*He picks up the valise and tosses it on his desk with a thud. Everyone flees in all directions.*) I will say, it's heavy for a rat trap. (*Now all alone, Oliver leans over with his ear to the case.*) Hickory Dickory Dock—the mouse ran up the clock. The clock struck one. BOOM! (*He trys the lock.*) Now, that's silly—to lock it. Who's going to steal a bomb.

(*He looks around for something to break the lock. He sees the revolver on his desk. He picks it up by the barrel to use as a hammer. But first, he listens again.*) Tick-tock-tick-tock-tick-tock. It's running faster. (*He begins to hammer away with the butt of the revolver.*) I never heard of a burglar-proof bomb before. Oh, well, there's one sure way to do it. (*He reverses the pistol and takes aim at the lock. He pulls the trigger. There is a click.*) Russian roulette. I forgot. Well, we'll try again. (*There is another click.*) That would have been Herbie. (*The next time there is the sound of a pistol shot and the lock flies off.*) That would have been me. (*Opens the top of the case.*) It's an exterminator alright. (*He takes out an alarm clock hooked to endless wires. Looks at the clock.*) Two minutes to one. I wonder if it has an alarm. (*He sets the clock on his desk and begins to pull endless lengths of wire out. Finally, he lifts out a batch of dynamite sticks tied together. Reads.*) "Handle with care. Dynamite." (*Places dynamite on desk.*) That's certainly the hard way to kill rats. (*Picks up clock again.*) One minute to one. It must be set for the one o'clock coffee break. (*He disconnects the wires. As he does so, the alarm rings. He jumps.*) Too late. (*He puts the clock down and calls.*) Come out—come out—wherever you are. (*The group returns—cautiously—from both sides.*)

BILL. Was it a bomb?

OLIVER. Set for one o'clock.

HERBIE. Is it safe?

OLIVER. I guess so. The alarm went off.

BILL. By George, that was the bravest thing I've ever seen.

MILLIE. You saved our lives.

HERBIE. And the bank.

SOPHIE. And my money.

OLIVER. What shall I do with this dynamite?

BILL. Be careful! Don't anybody smoke!

OLIVER. It's a filthy habit.

BILL. I'll take it out and give it to my sanitary disposal men.

MILLIE. Oh, Oliver. You could have been killed!

BILL. You got to give them credit. They tried. But we out-smarted them, Oliver. Didn't we, old boy?

OLIVER. We sure did, old boy.

BILL. And now they don't dare let you live. Alive—you're a luxury they can't afford.

OLIVER. Well, hardly anyone dead is a luxury.

BILL. Are we going to let them get away with this dastardly attempt, Oliver? NO!

OLIVER. No!

BILL. You know what we're going to do now, Oliver?

OLIVER. What?

BILL. We're going to call their bluff.

OLIVER. How?

BILL. I want you to walk right out that door and stand there to show them that you're still alive.

OLIVER. Won't they start shooting at me?

BILL. That's what I like about you, Oliver. You got a sharp mind.

OLIVER. You think they waited around?

BILL. Positive. They're parked in a sanitary disposal truck in front of the church.

OLIVER. Can't you give them a ticket?

BILL. We want to give them life.

OLIVER. What do I do when they start shooting?

BILL. Don't panic. Remember, we'll be out there, too.

OLIVER. Have you got enough men?

BILL. Fifty six. No—fifty five. One had to go to the dentist.

SOPHIE. I'm getting out of here.

BILL. No one leaves 'till the shooting's over.

SOPHIE. I left a pot roast on the stove.

BILL. Phone somebody. All right, Oliver. Give me five minutes to get my men set. What time is it?

OLIVER. Zero hour.

BILL. Let's synchronize our watches. I have five after one. What do you have?

OLIVER. Twelve thirty.

BILL. It's later than you think.

OLIVER. I know. Just think. Tonight I may never see the late late show.

MILLIE. Oliver! It's not worth it.

OLIVER. You don't know what's on.

BILL. We'll show those killers what you're made of. (*Goes to door.*) It may not take me five minutes. I'll blow my whistle. Then come out roaring like a lion.

MILLIE. Oliver, if you walk out that door to be killed, I'm going with you.

OLIVER. They're not waiting for you. You weren't invited.

MILLIE. Without you around, Oliver, I don't want to live.

SOPHIE. My pot roast is going to boil over.

OLIVER. No, Millie—you belong to Herbie.

HERBIE. I don't deserve her, Oliver. I give her to you.

SOPHIE. It'll stink up the house.

OLIVER. No, Herbie. I'm not worth it. I give her to you.

MILLIE. Stop giving me away! I want Oliver.

OLIVER. All right, Millie. Come outside in five minutes and you can have me. (*At this point, Anita comes running in the front door.*)

ANITA. Mister Pankey, I've got to see you.

OLIVER. Well, I'm rather busy at the moment. Could it wait five minutes?

ANITA. No. It's urgent.

OLIVER. Well, I can give you exactly four minutes and fifteen seconds.

ANITA. And personal.

OLIVER. (*To others.*) Would you folks mind waiting in the safety deposit vault?

MILLIE. Don't you go without me, Oliver. (*They go out.*)

OLIVER. Now, what is it, miss?

ANITA. I dreampt about you last night.

OLIVER. That's what you've got to tell me?

ANITA. Ever since I met you, I can't get you out of my mind.

OLIVER. I really don't think this is the time or place to go into anything like that.

ANITA. And when I woke up, I knew I had to see you.

OLIVER. Could you come back tomorrow?

ANITA. You seemed to haunt me.

OLIVER. You've picked a bad time, miss.

ANITA. And then I realized the truth. You're going to hate me.

OLIVER. I'm beginning to.

ANITA. You see, I know who you are.

OLIVER. A dead duck.

ANITA. You're John Doe.

OLIVER. Was that your dream?

ANITA. I suddenly placed you. You came in for a blood test.

OLIVER. And I got it.

ANITA. But it was a mistake, Mister Pankey.

OLIVER. It sure was. It's always best not to know the truth.

ANITA. You got the wrong report.

OLIVER. You mean I haven't got syphilis?

ANITA. You haven't got anything.

OLIVER. You mean—I'm healthy?

ANITA. You're healthier than the doctor.

OLIVER. You mean I'm not going to die?

ANITA. I'm terribly sorry.

OLIVER. I'm going to live?

ANITA. I'm afraid so.

OLIVER. You know what I'd like to do?

ANITA. Celebrate?

OLIVER. Hit you in the nose.

ANITA. We all make mistakes.

OLIVER. You don't know what you've put me thru?

ANITA. If there's anything I can do.

OLIVER. Yes—there is. (*Points.*) Go call Millie. Say there's something I've got to tell her. (*Anita goes out.*) I'm going to live! I'm going to live! (*Suddenly, a whistle can be heard. Oliver hears it. Realization dawns. He begins to tremble violently. Millie enters.*)

MILLIE. Oliver—what's the matter?

OLIVER. (*Moans.*) I'm going to live.

MILLIE. Why are you trembling?

OLIVER. I think I'm going to be sick.

MILLIE. Why?

OLIVER. Because I'm going to die.

MILLIE. What are you talking about?

OLIVER. I haven't got syphilis.

MILLIE. Well, I'm certainly glad to hear that.

OLIVER. You know what I've got?

MILLIE. What?

OLIVER. Three minutes.

MILLIE. You're not making very good sense, Oliver.

OLIVER. No, but I'm going to make a very good target. (*The whistle blows again. Oliver jumps a foot.*) Aah! That's for me.

MILLIE. Oliver, I've decided not to stand in your way. Who am I to stop you from being a hero?

OLIVER. Well, you could try, couldn't you?

MILLIE. I've got to show more faith in you. (*Picks up revolver.*) Face your destiny, Oliver.

OLIVER. EEK! That's a gun! (*Backs away.*) Put it down! It's loaded.

MILLIE. Don't you want it?

OLIVER. It might go off. Don't fool with it.

MILLIE. You're wonderful, Oliver. You want to go out there unarmed. (*Behind Oliver, a man enters with a violin case.*)

MAN. Excuse me, I'd like to cash a two dollar check.

OLIVER. (*Whirls around.*) Duck, Millie! They're after me!

MILLIE. Who's after you?

OLIVER. (*Points to man.*) That man's a killer.

MAN. I'm a musician.

OLIVER. (*Snatches up the pistol and holds it trembling violently.*) You got a gun in there.

MAN. I got a violin.

MILLIE. Oliver, that's Mister Poopouski from the Gypsy Tea Room. I know him.

OLIVER. You're a killer!

MAN. I'm Poopouski and His Sobbing Violin.

OLIVER. You don't fool me. Put that machine gun on the desk.

MAN. (*Follows instructions.*) What is it—a hold up?

OLIVER. Now, lie down on the floor.

MAN. (*Follows instructions.*) All of this trouble to cash a check?

MILLIE. Oliver, what's the matter with you?

OLIVER. Open that up, Millie. You'll find a gun inside. (*Millie opens case.*)

MAN. I think I'll change banks.

OLIVER. Well, is it a gun?

MILLIE. (*Looking down.*) No.

OLIVER. A violin?

MILLIE. No.

OLIVER. Well, what's in it?

MILLIE. (*Lifts up a shirt.*) Laundry.

MAN. I take it to the laundromat. A violin case looks better than a pillow case.

OLIVER. Oh. Well, this is a bank. It's no place to bring laundry.

MAN. (*Takes his case.*) I'll do it at home.

OLIVER. Cash his check, Millie.

MAN. Never mind. It's hardly worth the two dollars. (*He goes out.*)

MILLIE. Oliver, what's come over you!

OLIVER. Millie—I want to live.

MILLIE. Everybody wants to live.

OLIVER. But you don't understand. I want to live because I'm not going to die.

MILLIE. Everybody's got to die, too, Oliver.

OLIVER. But not in two minutes. (*The whistle blows again.*)

MILLIE. They're ready for you, Oliver.

OLIVER. They may be ready but I'm not. (*He crawls under his desk to hide.*)

MILLIE. Oliver, what are you looking for?

OLIVER. An aspirin. (*Bill comes in the front door.*)

BILL. Where the hell is Oliver?

MILLIE. Under his desk.

BILL. What's he doing under there?

MILLIE. Looking for an aspirin.

BILL. (*Peers under desk.*) What's the matter, Oliver? Did your watch stop?

OLIVER. No. My heart.

BILL. We're all waiting for you out there.

OLIVER. (*Sticks head out.*) I know. They're waiting for me up there, too. (*Points heavenward.*)

BILL. Are you coming out?

OLIVER. You mean today?

BILL. Didn't you hear me whistle?

OLIVER. I thought it was my breathing.

BILL. Is anything wrong with you?

OLIVER. I think I'm paralyzed.

BILL. Shall I send some one in?

OLIVER. Yes. A priest.

BILL. I know. You're playing a game.

OLIVER. Cat and mouse.

BILL. You're holding up the whole shooting match, Oliver.

OLIVER. Don't tell me!

BILL. Are you backing out?

OLIVER. Not from under here.

BILL. (*Straightens up.*) I know what he wants.

OLIVER. A good night's sleep.

BILL. (*To Millie.*) He just wants a word alone with you under there. Well, give him a kiss and send him out. (*He goes out.*)

MILLIE. You want me under there with you, Oliver?

OLIVER. I've got to come out. I'm getting a cramp. (*He crawls out.*)

MILLIE. Oliver, what's happened?

OLIVER. Millie—all this time I thought I was going to die. The doctor made a mistake. So I didn't care. But now, I've just found out that I'm going to live.

MILLIE. But that's wonderful, Oliver.

OLIVER. It's terrible. Because I've got to die anyhow.

MILLIE. Why?

OLIVER. I rented a car for six months. I've bought jewelry and suits and an electric toothbrush.

MILLIE. What's wrong with that?

OLIVER. I've got to pay for them.

MILLIE. Why worry? Nobody else does.

OLIVER. But my mother isn't on Social Security yet. If I die I can pay my debts.

MILLIE. Oliver, your life is worth more than your debts.

OLIVER. Not to *Hertz-Rent-a-Car*.

MILLIE. You mean you're going out there to be shot at just to pay for an electric toothbrush?

OLIVER. I've got to. And I'm afraid.

MILLIE. A man like you? A man that bit a gorilla?

OLIVER. I've got no choice now.

MILLIE. Do you want to die?

OLIVER. No. But I need the reward.

MILLIE. Are you scared?

OLIVER. I'm scared to death. Look at my hand shake. I couldn't even hold a drink. Even if I drank.

MILLIE. Then you're a brave man, Oliver. It's not brave to risk your life when you want to die. It's only brave when you want to live.

OLIVER. Tell that to my mother. Goodbye, Millie. Marry Herbie and be happy. Name the first boy after me.

MILLIE. I will, Oliver. Even if it's a girl.

OLIVER. I'm glad I splurged on silk jockey shorts. I'll look better when they undress me.

MILLIE. You'll come out of this alive, Oliver. But if you don't, I'm going to become a nun.

OLIVER. You do that, Millie. They're dressing better nowadays. (*He goes out on wobbly legs. There is a long wait. Then we hear the sudden bark of machine guns. Millie flinches. She kneels down to pray. In a moment, McSwain and the officer enter carrying Oliver by his arms and legs. They lower him to the floor.)*

OFFICER. Well, it's over.

BILL. He'll get the reward he wanted.

MILLIE. Tell me—was his last word—Millie?

OFFICER. No. "Ouch."

MILLIE. He died the way he wanted to die—in silk jockey shorts.

OFFICER. I never looked.

BILL. He'll be all right.

MILLIE. What do you mean—he'll be all right?

OFFICER. Lucky thing he fainted when he did. Gave us a chance to get them first.

BILL. There's nothing the matter with him.

MILLIE. Then what's he doing dead?

BILL. Hit his head on a fire plug.

OFFICER. Give him a minute—he'll be all right. *(They start out.)*

BILL. What a guy! What guts!

OFFICER. What a target. *(Goes out. Millie kneels beside Oliver and cradles his head in her lap.)*

MILLIE. Oliver Wendell Pankey—my hero. *(Oliver opens his eyes and looks slowly around.)*

OLIVER. Heaven is a bank?

MILLIE. They got the bandits, Oliver. And you'll get a reward. And you're not dead, Oliver.

OLIVER. How can you tell?

MILLIE. *(Kisses him.)* There. Are you dead?

OLIVER. *(Blinks uncertainly.)* Ask me again. *(As she kisses him again, the curtain falls.)*

CURTAIN

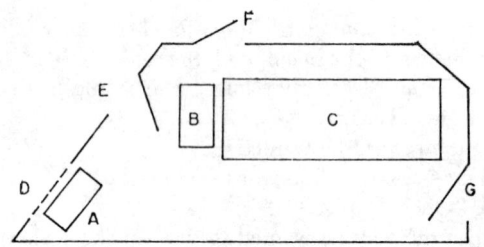

SCENE DESIGN: SMALL BEDROOM (ACT I, SCENE I) (ACT 2, SCENE 2)

A. CHAIR   E. CLOTHES CLOSET
B. END TABLE   F. BATH DOOR
C. SOFA BED   G. ENTRANCE
D. WINDOW

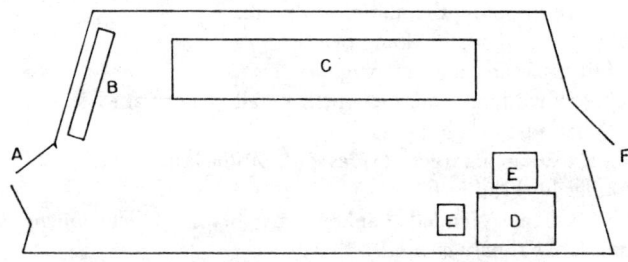

SCENE DESIGN: BANK, (ACT I SCENES 2 & 4) (ACT 2 SCENES 1 & 3)

A. DOUBLE DOORS
B. WRITING STAND
C. TELLERS CAGES
D. DESK
E. CHAIRS
F. DOOR

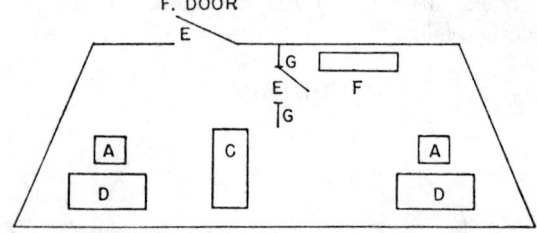

SCENE DESIGN: DIVIDED OFFICE (ACT I, SCENE 3)

A. CHAIRS   F. FILE
D. DESKS   G. PARTIAL PARTITION
E. DOORS
C. BENCH

80

PROPERTY PLOT

Radio
Alarm clock
Hot plate
Coke bottles
Eye mask
Glasses
Bottle and pills
Water glass
Tea kettle
Towels
Suitcase
Shorts
Electric shaver
Switch blade knife
Shirts
Wrist watches
Engagement ring
Wallet, with traffic tickets
Paper money
Toothbrush
Shopping cart
Money bags
Pencil and paper
Pennies
Cigarettes and lighter
Magazines
Wall mirror
Cabinet file
(2) desks
Sofa-bed
Box of "bees"

Medical forms
Book
Newspaper
FBI badge
Sandwich
Stethoscope
Coins
Phone book
Violin case, with laundry
Waste basket
Telephone
Hi-fi set
Washroom keys
Revolver
Mask
Needle and thread
Button
Vase and flowers
Cut-out dummy
Tray and breakfast
Fan letters
Blouse
Bottle
Valise
Dynamite (substitute auto flare)
Alarm clock (interior with wires)
Alarm bell
Police whistle
Assorted mail
Bank forms

TODAY'S HOTTEST NEW PLAYS

❑ **THREE VIEWINGS by Jeffrey Hatcher.** Three comic-dramatic monologues, set in a midwestern funeral parlor, interweave as they explore the ways we grieve, remember, and move on. *"Finally, what we have been waiting for: a new, true, idiosyncratic voice in the theater. And don't tell me you hate monologues; you can't hate them more than I do. But these are much more: windows into the deep of each speaker's fascinating, paradoxical, unique soul, and windows out into a gallery of surrounding people, into hilarious and horrific coincidences and conjunctions, into the whole dirty but irresistible business of living in this damnable but spellbinding place we presume to call the world."* - New York Magazine. [1M, 2W]

❑ **HAVING OUR SAY by Emily Mann.** The Delany Sisters' Bestselling Memoir is now one of Broadway's Best-Loved Plays! Having lived over one hundred years apiece, Bessie and Sadie Delany have plenty to say, and their story is not simply African-American history or women's history...it is our history as a nation. *"The most provocative and entertaining family play to reach Broadway in a long time."* - New York Times. *"Fascinating, marvelous, moving and forceful."* - Associated Press. [2W]

❑ **THE YOUNG MAN FROM ATLANTA Winner of the 1995 Pulitzer Prize. by Horton Foote.** An older couple attempts to recover from the suicide death of their only son, but the menacing truth of why he died, and what a certain Young Man from Atlanta had to do with it, keeps them from the peace they so desperately need. *"Foote ladles on character and period nuances with a density unparalleled in any living playwright."* - NY Newsday. [5M, 4W]

❑ **SIMPATICO by Sam Shepard.** Years ago, two men organized a horse racing scam. Now, years later, the plot backfires against the ringleader when his partner decides to come out of hiding. *"Mr. Shepard writing at his distinctive, savage best."* - New York Times. [3M, 3W]

❑ **MOONLIGHT by Harold Pinter.** The love-hate relationship between a dying man and his family is the subject of Harold Pinter's first full-length play since *Betrayal*. *"Pinter works the language as a master pianist works the keyboard."* - New York Post. [4M, 2W, 1G]

❑ **SYLVIA by A.R. Gurney.** This romantic comedy, the funniest to come along in years, tells the story of a twenty-two year old marriage on the rocks, and of Sylvia, the dog who turns it all around. *"A delicious and dizzy new comedy."* - New York Times. *"FETCHING! I hope it runs longer than Cats!"* - New York Daily News. [2M, 2W]

DRAMATISTS PLAY SERVICE, INC.
440 Park Avenue South, New York, New York 10016 212-683-8960 Fax 212-213-1539

TODAY'S HOTTEST NEW PLAYS

☐ **MOLLY SWEENEY by Brian Friel, Tony Award-Winning Author of *Dancing at Lughnasa*.** Told in the form of monologues by three related characters, *Molly Sweeney* is mellifluous, Irish storytelling at its dramatic best. Blind since birth, Molly recounts the effects of an eye operation that was intended to restore her sight but which has unexpected and tragic consequences. *"Brian Friel has been recognized as Ireland's greatest living playwright. Molly Sweeney confirms that Mr. Friel still writes like a dream. Rich with rapturous poetry and the music of rising and falling emotions...Rarely has Mr. Friel written with such intoxicating specificity about scents, colors and contours." - New York Times.* [2M, 1W]

☐ **SWINGING ON A STAR (The Johnny Burke Musical) by Michael Leeds. 1996 Tony Award Nominee for Best Musical.** The fabulous songs of Johnny Burke are perfectly represented here in a series of scenes jumping from a 1920s Chicago speakeasy to a World War II USO Show and on through the romantic high jinks of the Bob Hope/Bing Crosby "Road Movies." Musical numbers include such favorites as "Pennies from Heaven," "Misty," "Ain't It a Shame About Mame," "Like Someone in Love," and, of course, the Academy Award winning title song, "Swinging on a Star." *"A WINNER. YOU'LL HAVE A BALL!" - New York Post. "A dazzling, toe-tapping, finger-snapping delight!" - ABC Radio Network. "Johnny Burke wrote his songs with moonbeams!" - New York Times.* [3M, 4W]

☐ **THE MONOGAMIST by Christopher Kyle.** Infidelity and mid-life anxiety force a forty-something poet to reevaluate his 60s values in a late 80s world. *"THE BEST COMEDY OF THE SEASON. Trenchant, dark and jagged. Newcomer Christopher Kyle is a playwright whose social satire comes with a nasty, ripping edge - Molière by way of Joe Orton." - Variety. "By far the most stimulating playwright I've encountered in many a buffaloed moon." - New York Magazine. "Smart, funny, articulate and wisely touched with rue...the script radiates a bright, bold energy." - The Village Voice.* [2M, 3W]

☐ **DURANG/DURANG by Christopher Durang.** These cutting parodies of *The Glass Menagerie* and *A Lie of the Mind*, along with the other short plays in the collection, prove once and for all that Christopher Durang is our theater's unequivocal master of outrageous comedy. *"The fine art of parody has returned to theater in a production you can sink your teeth and mind into, while also laughing like an idiot." - New York Times. "If you need a break from serious drama, the place to go is Christopher Durang's silly, funny, over-the-top sketches." - TheatreWeek.* [3M, 4W, flexible casting]

DRAMATISTS PLAY SERVICE, INC.
440 Park Avenue South, New York, New York 10016 212-683-8960 Fax 212-213-1539